The B&C Discography: 1968 to 1975

Action, Stable, B&C, Pegasus, Peg, Mooncrest, People, Dragon, Sussex & Seven Sun

The B&C Discography: 1968 to 1975

Action, Stable, B&C, Pegasus, Peg, Mooncrest, People, Dragon, Sussex & Seven Sun

Mark Jones

This edition published 2013 by

The Record Press

The Record Press is an imprint of Bristol Folk Publications
www.bristol–folk.co.uk

ISBN 978-0-9563531-7-7

Copyright © Mark Clinton Jones 2013

The right of Mark Clinton Jones to be identified as the Author of this work has been asserted in accordance with the Copyrights, Designs and Patents Act 1988.

Cover design copyright © Mark Clinton Jones 2013

All rights reserved. No part of this book may be reprinted or reproduced or utilised or transmitted in any form or by any means, electronic or mechanical, including photocopy, recording, or any information storage and retrieval system, including the Internet, now known or hereafter invented, without permission in writing from the copyright holder.

Layout, design and digital realisation by Bristol Folk Publications.
Printed and bound in the EU by Lulu.com.

The B&C Discography: 1968 to 1975

Contents

Introduction......1
B&C Records Ltd. – a short history......3
Introduction to the discographies......17
    Label designs......17
    Pressing companies used by B&C......17
    Sources used in lists......18
    Release and deletion dates......18
    Recommended retail price......19
Discographies......20
   Action......20
    ACLP/ACLS sequence LPs......20
    ACMP sequence LP......23
    ACT 4500 sequence 7" singles......23
    ACT 4600 sequence 7" singles......27
    ACT 100 sequence 7" singles......29
    Promotional 7" EP......29
   Stable......30
    SLP sequence LP......30
    SLE sequence LPs......30
    STA sequence 7" single......31
    Promotional 7" EP......31
   B&C and Charisma......32
    CAS sequence LPs......32
    BCB sequence LP......40
    BCM sequence LPs......41
    CB sequence 7" singles......42
    Promotional 7" singles......49
   Pegasus and Peg......51
    PEG sequence LPs......51
    PS sequence LPs......53
    Tape versions of CAS sequence LPs......54
    PGS sequence 7" singles......54
    Promotional 7" records......55
   Mooncrest......56
    CREST sequence LPs......56
    MOON sequence 7" singles......62
   People......66
    PLEO sequence LPs......66
    PLED sequence double LP......70
    PLE sequence tape–only release......71
    PEO sequence 7" singles......71
    Promotional 7" EP......73
   Dragon......74
    DRLS sequence LPs......74
    DRA sequence 7" singles......75
   Sussex......79
    LPSX sequence LPs......79
    LPDX sequence double LP......81
    SSX sequence 7" singles......81
   Seven Sun......82
    SSUN sequence 7" singles......82
   And finally......83
    A last–ditch cross–label tape–only hits package......83

Introduction

This book had its beginnings in a combination of *The Famous Charisma Discography* and a spin–off article for *Record Collector*. Feedback from both was pleasantly positive, but what surprised me was the number of suggestions that I should follow these up with a book on B&C. For a couple of years I avoided the idea on the basis that I didn't know enough about the company to produce anything worthwhile – what I knew about B&C was mostly in its relationship with Charisma. However, a trawl through unused research materials reminded me that I'd gathered lots of information on Stable, Pegasus, Peg and Mooncrest so from point of view of discographical content there was more than enough to make a B&C discography viable. It didn't take long to find out that Action, People, Sussex and Seven Sun had also been members of the B&C stable. The decision was made – *The B&C Discography* would be the second book in the '*Light Engine*' sub–series.

For a short while a madness took hold and I considered including Trojan and all related labels – Ackee, Amalgamated, Ashanti, Attack, Big, Big Shot, Blue Cat, Bread, Clandisc, Coxsone, Down Town, Duke, Duke Reid, Dynamic, Explosion, Gayfeet, GG, Grape, Green Door, Harry J, High Note, Horse, Hot Rod, J–Dan, Jackpot, Joe, Moodisc, Pressure Beat, Randy's, Smash, Song Bird, Studio One, Summit, Tabernacle, Techniques, Treasure Isle and Upsetter. Thank goodness that common sense came to the rescue in time.

So, barring Charisma, of which more in a second, this book covers all of B&C's non–reggae labels. The Dragon label is the exception that proves the rule and is included because it was a subsidiary of Mooncrest rather than of Trojan. Charisma releases are only included for the three catalogue number sequences that were shared with B&C, and that only up to the final B&C release on each sequence. This is because comprehensive information on all B&C–era Charisma releases already exists in *The Famous Charisma Discography* and to duplicate swathes of that book seemed silly. On one hand it would have doubled the size and cost of this book, whilst on the other the last thing I wanted to do was cannibalise sales of the Charisma book – after all, I'm still living in the hope of making back the production costs for the bloody thing one day.

So why no pictures? Well, it's all down to copyright and cost. From experience, I know that negotiating to reproduce sleeves can add years to a project and incur silly costs – e.g. EMI once tried to charge me £1,000 (plus VAT) to reproduce fifteen Wurzels sleeves. I didn't take them up on the offer. Universal/Sanctuary is a much happier company to deal with, but the problem is that although they own these labels, they don't own copyright on all of the sleeve designs because these were often licensed in one–off deals along with the music. For sleeves and labels try *discogs.com* and the exemplary *45cat.com*.

Thanks to

Al Fenn for information on Decameron's lost releases (and Johnny Coppin for putting me in touch); Record Collector's Ian Shirley for encouragement; fellow Charisma sleuth hounds, Mike Clayton and Steve Trump for corrections and additions to the Charisma volume; last but not least, Colin Richardson, head of Charisma/B&C's International Department, for some great stuff that I couldn't print about his B&C opposite number's persistent attempts to spend company money on unnecessary foreign jaunts. Well, what's an International Department for is what I say?

B&C Records Ltd. – a short history

To say that the B&C group of companies is particularly difficult to research has more than a hint of understatement about it. B&C's prime mover, Lee Gopthal, was, over the years, director of – or otherwise had one or more fingers in – a bewildering number of companies, including rivals, and the number of labels owned or marketed by B&C comes in at around the fifty mark. B&C is mostly remembered on the record collecting scene for its affiliations with Trojan and Charisma, but the company was originally set up in association with Island, with which company it retained very close links until 1972, when the jointly–run Trojan label passed solely to B&C. Although this book is not concerned with Trojan and its myriad number of sub–labels, the organisational history would be misleading, not to mention even more confusing, if it did not include Trojan's operations to some extent. Indeed, at the end of the day, B&C and Trojan went down together and, retaining all assets but minus all liabilities, both companies were resurrected together. That's going a bit too far ahead, though – this book is concerned only with events prior to B&C's liquidation in 1975, though subsequent events are covered briefly just to tie up some otherwise loose ends.

A convenient place to begin the story is on board the Ministry of Transport ship, *Empire Windrush*, in 1948. On 21 June of that year the *Empire Windrush* arrived at Tilbury with the first group of Caribbean migrants to the UK on board. Amongst this group was Sikarum Gopthal, who was described as a "Mechanic" on the passenger inventory[1]. His proposed address was ambiguously listed as "East Croydon". Whether he found work as a mechanic is unknown, but by 1952 he was in business as a tailor, working from a shop at 108, Cambridge Road, Kilburn, NW6. In November 1952 Sikarum's thirteen year old son, Leichman, or Lee, as he was known, left Jamaica for the UK and moved into the flat above his father's shop. Not much is known of subsequent years until, when age allowed, he joined a firm of certified accountants and studied toward professional qualifications.

In the early 1960s Sikarum returned to Jamaica by which time Lee had secured a mortgage on 108, Cambridge Road. He sought tenants to help with repayments and the first in was Sonny Roberts. Roberts built the UK's first black–owned recording studio in the basement and released records on his own Planetone and Swan labels. This venture lasted until 1963 and Planetone records from that year included the Cambridge Road address on labels. The next set of tenants would expand the building's musical operations. In May 1962, Island Records relocated from Jamaica to the UK. To begin with the company ran its UK operations from Chris Blackwell's flat at 4, Rutland Gate Mews, SW7 but Island soon needed more space and moved into the ground floor shop at Cambridge Road late in 1962. Blackwell, along with new Island recruit, David Betteridge, was keen for Gopthal to become involved with Island, presumably because of the combination of his Jamaican origin and his knowledge of accountancy practices.

Initially, the trio considered setting up a purely mail order sales channel. However, Gopthal suggested that door–to–door sales would be a better way to sell records to the now well–established West Indian community, so Gopthal and Island advertised for salesmen. By early 1963 Gopthal had put together the team that was to become the core of B&C and its related companies over the next twelve years – namely Jim Flynn, Barry Creasy, Alan Firth and Fred Parsons. In all, sixteen salesmen were run from Gopthal's bedroom. Of the rest of 108, Cambridge Road, all of the rooms were by now let, mostly to Island. The record selling business was formalised with the incorporation of Beat &

The B&C Discography: 1968 to 1975

Commercial Records Ltd. on 19 April 1963[2]. However, Gopthal did not want to give up his accountancy career and considered Beat and Commercial and his involvement with Island to be part time ventures only. It was Island's success with Millie's *My Boy Lollipop* in March 1964 that enticed Gopthal into the music business full time.

By 1966 Gopthal, Blackwell and Betteridge wanted to complement their current salesmen–based distribution operations by opening a retail outlet, so the first Musicland shop was opened in Willesden Lane, Kilburn[3]. Gopthal worked in the shop whilst Blackwell and Betteridge concentrated on running Island and licensing records from Jamaica. By 1967 there were seven Musicland outlets including a mail order outlet and a market stall. Of Gopthal's original partners, Creasy and Firth became directors of Musicland, whilst Flynn and Parsons became directors of Beat and Commercial.

In 1968 came an unexpected requirement for change. The local council informed Gopthal that 108, Cambridge Road was going to be demolished for road widening. Gopthal and Betteridge somewhat hurriedly set about finding a new base for operations. They chose 12, Neasden Lane, Willesden, NW10, which had previously been used by the mail order company, New Fairway House Ltd. Island and Beat and Commercial moved in and, rather grandly, gave their new home the name 'Music House'. Rob Bell, who worked for Island and, later, Trojan, described Music House thus:

> ... there was a parking area in front of the long rectangular building that held at least eight cars. One walked in through the front door into a reception area which was to the right ... Doreen, [the Receptionist] sat next to a manual switchboard – one of those intriguing artefacts of telephonic days gone by – dexterously switching jack ended cables. To the left of the reception area, but to the centre of the building a corridor ran up the length of the structure, with offices on each side. The first offices were used by Lee Gopthal and his B&C crew, Jim Flynn, Barry Creasy, Allan [sic] Firth and Fred Parsons. The largest space on the left was a storeroom/warehouse for the Musicland operation, and the last door on the right led into the first Island office which was [David Betteridge's]. He had a large table around which sat Jill Grant, and whichever of the three van reps might be in the building ... The door at the top of the corridor led into the general Island office, with telephone sales, accountancy etc. John Leftly, the accountant [also a board member] had an office to the right of the main office, and then another door led past two more accounting offices into the warehouse area behind.[4]

The two companies found working together to be synergistic – Island had a distribution network of vans driven by knowledgeable reps, sales contacts up and down the country plus contacts and contracts with Jamaican producers, whilst B&C, as Beat and Commercial had started to call itself, was expanding its Musicland retail base. Music House was the hub of operations for both the B&C and Island group of companies and the average day sounds somewhat hectic – Rob Bell again:

> ... trucks would be delivering product from Orlake [one of the pressing companies used by Island and B&C], orders would be pulled for the Island reps. for the Musicland stores who ordered very large amounts, and there would be a constant stream of retailers, some easy to deal with, and others beset by endless credit hassles who seemed to be constantly wading through swamps of poverty and adversity in general ... Gopthal would come in with a huge order ... and say he needed them to be ready by 6 o'clock that evening – in 45 minutes time. In the

background would be the whirring of the Pitney Bowes postage machine as orders were being franked for a run to the post office in twenty minutes, just in time to catch the mail. These would have been orders that had come in after the Post Office mail van had already called for and collected the bulk of that day's mail orders. Piles of albums and forty fives were stacked on rolling carts, or sat in piles between the shelves. Deliveries that had come in during the day, but had not yet been put away. New releases often came in and went out so fast it was pointless to shelve them in the appropriate area. Right then, right where they were was the appropriate area. And over all this mayhem boomed the sound of reggae – there was always time to keep the turntables turning. After the big orders had been pulled and collected or delivered, the mail had gone, and Steve or someone took a last trip to one of the big railway stations to ship by Red Star orders to Dave Bloxham or HR Taylor[5], the midlands distributor, a relative calm descended upon Music House.[6]

Based on Island's example and visible success, Gopthal began striking his own deals with Jamaican producers. An advert placed by B&C in the US music trade magazine, *Billboard*, listed its labels as Action, Amalgamated, Blue Cat, Coxsome [sic] and Tabernacle and went on to say, "Our Retail Division Is Musicland" and that there were now, "Fourteen Branches in London and Suburbs"[7].

However, just as Gopthal was throwing himself into the distribution of Jamaican music, Island was in the process of realigning itself with British pop music. Chris Blackwell had recently discovered how much more income could be derived from white groups, such as the Spencer Davis Group, which didn't just sell large numbers of singles, but also sold LPs in large quantities. Jamaican music tended to be single, rather than LP, oriented, hence missing out on the increased income that could be derived from selling the more lucrative LP format. Chris Blackwell later said:

> It was the end of an era and the beginning of a new one ... Up until then I had spent 75 per cent of my time on Jamaican music and only 25 per cent on pop and rock. I realised it was time to reverse that.[8]

So, with the decision to align with white, British music, Island sold most of its subsidiary labels to Gopthal. However, at the same time, Blackwell, at Gopthal's suggestion, resurrected the dormant Trojan label[9], which became a 50/50 venture between Island and B&C. Island decided to use its West Indies Pop (WIP) 7" catalogue sequence specifically for its British pop output, plus the more obviously commercial of the Jamaican releases, whilst the West Indian (WI) sequence releases were switched to Trojan. The original directors of Trojan were, from B&C/Musicland, Gopthal and Alan Firth plus Island's Graham Walker. B&C's Fred Parsons and Jim Flynn (not forgetting Tilly the secretary) completed Trojan's original staff and, later in the year, Island's Rob Bell moved across to Trojan. At some point, Island's Dave Bloxham also moved to Trojan to work with B&C's Clive Crawley on radio promotion – or 'plugging' as it was commonly known.

On the publishing front, B&C Music Ltd. was incorporated just in time for credits to appear on the first new Trojan release (TR 601)[10]. *Billboard*, in a later article on independent UK record companies, stated that B&C Music was run by Lionel Conway at Island Music[11] Of those reggae labels now run by B&C, many of the earlier Coxsone releases from 1967 and Amalgamated releases from early 1968 had been published by Island Music, but once B&C Music was incorporated, this new credit started to appear comprehensively on B&C releases and on Trojan's expanding number of record labels.

Lee Gopthal had obviously learned from Island's example of gaining UK publishing rights on Jamaican product and that spreading the load via numerous limited liability companies looked like a good way of ensuring that if one company went down, then there would still be others to provide income. Either that or the whole lot would collapse like a house of cards. But we're looking into the future here.

Trojan, along with its subsidiary labels, began to operate in a near monopoly on the reggae front as rival labels went under or were absorbed into the B&C group of companies. The thinking behind the creation of so many label imprints was that there was too much product from various producers to be released purely on Trojan. Therefore, distinct labels were created for different producers, with Trojan often cherry–picking the best of the crop – or at least, cherry–picking those records considered to have more commercial appeal, which may not be quite the same thing.

B&C's first non–Jamaican label was Action, which continued, with one or two gaps in service, until B&C's eventual liquidation in 1975. It is odd that this label was first listed in the May 1968 *Billboard* advert mentioned earlier because Action's first release did not appear until around September of that year. The label was formed by noted blues authority, John Abbey, who, along with Bob Kilborn, also produced *Blues and Soul* magazine. Action licensed and released American R&B for the majority of its existence, but was resurrected in 1975 under the aegis of Webster Shrowder as an 'ethnic' reggae label.

Next up on the label front was Stable, which was added to the B&C Group in late 1968 and provided the first home–grown British music for the company. Stable was run by Simon Stable, who wrote the 'Droppings from the Stable' feature in *International Times*. Oddly, in *Billboard*, a regular article on goings–on in London stated that "The independent Action Stable company has changed its name to B and C Records"[12]. This piece of erroneous news was probably down to the recent formation of the B&C Records Ltd. record company as distinct from the Beat and Commercial Records Ltd. record retail company. Meanwhile, Music House expanded to take in the next door garage so as to cope with Island's increasingly successful LP operations.

It should be mentioned that B&C Records Ltd. was not based at Music House but was, for its whole existence, at 37 Soho Square, London W1[13]. Proceedings on the new B&C label were kicked off in May 1969 with a Merrill Moore single, produced by Action's John Abbey in Los Angeles. To begin with, B&C Records Ltd. continued in the Action mould of licensing US music for UK release, though it soon started to achieve something of an identity crisis by releasing soft reggae and contemporary UK pop, rock and folk.

At some point during 1969, Lee Gopthal had a meeting with Tony Stratton Smith, who managed The Nice, The Bonzo Dog Band and Van der Graaf Generator. The reason behind this particular meeting is lost in the mists of time – perhaps it was Musicland business, because Stratton–Smith is known to have been involved in the retail side of the music business during the 1960s. Gopthal knew that Stratton Smith was frustrated with the various record companies to which his artists were signed, so suggested that he start his own record company in partnership with B&C, who would "handle sales and marketing"[14]. Perhaps this was serendipity, because Charisma's Gail Colson points out that Stratton Smith had already been thinking about setting up a record company:

> I cannot for the life of me remember how Tony met up with Lee Gopthal and B&C – but somewhere along the way he did ... we had the name

Charisma and the whole idea of starting a record company way before he came on the scene.[15]

The upshot of this was that Stratton Smith wrote to Gopthal on 15th October, 1969, with a letter of intent to enter "… into an agreement with B&C Records Limited to launch a label to be known as, 'CHARISMA RECORDS', Charisma being a Trade Mark of Stratton Smith Music Ltd."[16]

With B&C handling sales and marketing a close working relationship was formed between the companies, which went so far as to include Lee Gopthal as one of Charisma's directors. It also included Charisma sharing B&C's main LP catalogue number sequence (until late 1971) and its single catalogue sequence (until late 1972), which was the cause of much confusion in trade publications. Later on the companies became even closer – literally – when Charisma moved in to B&C's Soho Square address. The two companies were even close to merging at one point, though this did not eventually come about – more of which later.

Meanwhile, the current distribution set up that B&C and Island had with Philips/Phonodisc wasn't working as well as it might on the Trojan and Action fronts. Apart from the few reggae records that made the charts and so achieved mainstream UK sales, the majority of Trojan releases sold within West Indian enclaves, as did the majority of Action's soul material. Philips' distribution services couldn't service these more parochial needs because it was geared to more mainstream national distribution. Island and B&C came to an agreement with Philips to allow localised distribution via Birmingham's Keith Prowse and H.R. Taylor companies. Island's David Betteridge explained, "The Specialization of these two independent distributors will give us a wider and better distribution of our Trojan product ... but Philips and Phonodisc will hold on to a few major Trojan releases."[17] The average sales for a release on Trojan or one of its associated labels was generally between 3,000 and 4,000[18] and many customers only wanted a song whilst it was still 'hot' in the clubs, so getting the records to the right place at the right time was essential, hence the need for more specialised distribution services.

In June 1970, *The London Gazette* included notice of the possible winding up of Musicland Ltd., which started a confusing series of events on B&C's retail side. Musicland Ltd. was not wound up (at this point, at least) but to confuse the issue, Beat & Commercial Records Ltd. changed its name to Musicland Record Stores Ltd. on 29 July, 1970. Presumably it had been confusing having two companies within the group – Beat & Commercial Records Ltd. and B&C Records Ltd. – sharing the same acronym. In 1971, Musicland Ltd. and Musicland Record Stores Ltd. were joined by the Muzik City chain of shops. These were set up specifically to service a black consumer base and specialised, according to contemporary adverts, in reggae and soul plus jazz imports – with "pop" placed very firmly at the bottom of the list. Muzik City's head office was listed in adverts as being in Music House, which must have been getting very crowded by now.

In April 1972, the directors of Musicland Ltd. were listed as Gopthal, Jim Flynn, Fred Parsons, Barry Creasy and Alan Firth along with Island's David Betteridge and Chris Blackwell. By the look of things, Island pulled out of the company soon after this because a report of the sale of the company listed the directors as comprising only Gopthal, Creasy and Firth[19]. Musicland Ltd. was sold to the rival Scene and Heard chain of record shops, which was owned by Syad Ali. The article stated that a new umbrella company would be formed to run both Musicland and Scene and Heard and that the directors of this company would be Gopthal, Ali and Firth. Seemingly to confuse matters even further (if that were possible) during 1972 Music City Ltd., Muzik City Record Shops Ltd. and Trojanland Ltd. were all incorporated and Gopthal was listed on the board of directors for each. Which, if any, of these was formed as the umbrella company for Musicland and Scene and Heard is unknown. Musicland Ltd. was eventually dissolved in 1973 and Musicland Record Stores Ltd. continued until 1977, when it too was dissolved.

Moving back to the B&C label, to try to give contemporary British rock and folk artists signed to B&C a more consistent image, the Pegasus label was formed in 1971. Atomic Rooster, Andy Roberts and Steeleye Span were transferred from B&C to the new imprint and at least two LPs originally earmarked for B&C were given a 'free transfer' to Pegasus instead. However, Pegasus didn't last long under this name. The story goes that an American label threatened legal action unless the label name was changed, which might, if true, explain how the label name was quietly shortened to Peg in 1972. Once Pegasus was started no further B&C LPs were issued on the full price CAS catalogue sequence, which was now used exclusively by Charisma. B&C continued to release singles on the shared CB sequence as well as releasing budget–priced rock 'n' roll revival LPs on its BCM sequence.

Talking of rock 'n' roll revival, there were plans afoot to create a label especially dedicated to this genre, though as a label imprint of Trojan rather than B&C. *Billboard* reported: "It is understood that [Trojan is] contemplating the introduction of a label which will be devoted to rock 'n' roll. Tentative name for the label is Wild Cat."[20] This label did not materialise, perhaps because there was already a Swedish rock 'n' roll label called Wildcat and records in this genre continued to be issued on B&C on both the BCM and CB sequences. The last B&C release on the CB sequence was CB 190, after which the sequence was used purely by Charisma until that label's demise in 1987. At the tail end of 1972, however, both the new Peg label and the old B&C label were discontinued when B&C Records Ltd. metamorphosed from a record label into a marketing company[21].

By late 1972, Island, had already disentangled itself from B&C's retail operations and had ceased to act as distributor for B&C–related record labels[22]. The process of breaking completely with B&C continued in October, when B&C became sole owners of Trojan, and in November, when Island left Music House to move into a new, purpose–built warehouse in Brentford[23]. Lee Gopthal, sensibly, took this opportunity to retrench and started to prune Trojan, both in terms of the number of sub labels and also in terms of artist roster. The plan was that by the end of the year only Horse, Big Shot, Explosion, Green Door and Attack would remain from Trojan's forty or so sub labels[24].

With Island easing itself out of the picture, it looks as though Gopthal quickly started thinking in terms of creating closer ties between B&C and the increasingly successful Charisma label. The first inkling of these plans came in June 1972 with news of the alignment of Charisma's and B&C's various music publishing companies:

> Although the exact details of the B&C merger with Tony Stratton Smith's Charisma label have still to be announced, both companies' music publishing activities have now been joined together under the management of Mike de Haviland [sic], previously Charisma's promotion manager.[25]

Mike de Havilland[26] had set up Mooncrest Music for Charisma in early 1972 and he now took over management of Brewer Music, one of Charisma's publishing companies, plus

The B&C Discography: 1968 to 1975

Trojan Music and B&C Music, which he now ran alongside Mooncrest Music. Mooncrest Music, after this closer alignment with B&C, later gained sub–publishing rights to Rasta Music, Ginlor Music and Lobek Music[27].

Early in 1973 the Mooncrest record label was set up with Lee Gopthal and Tony Stratton Smith as directors. However, with a confusing mishmash of heavy rock[28], bubblegum pop, light reggae and folk–based music, the whole Mooncrest set up, whatever the aims stated below for the label, looked suspiciously like the old B&C label in all but name. *Billboard* presented quite an in–depth feature on the formation of the label:

> Mooncrest, a joint venture label backed by the B&C–Charisma companies, will function as a "quality" pop label, thus broadening the creative base of the two companies' major involvement in the reggae and contemporary fields ... [The label's first releases will be] singles by Nazareth, Python Lee (formerly Python Lee Jackson) with Dana Gillespie as lead singer, and A and A North, 20–year–old Welsh twin brothers, who are produced by songwriter Ronnie Scott. On the same date, two albums will be released – "Razamanaz" by Nazareth and "Sunny days" by the Canadian band Lighthouse. Nazareth is a former B&C act, as is another of Mooncrest's first signings, Welsh singer Ritchie Francis[29]. Also contracted to the new label is eight–year–old Donna Newman from Manchester, who has recently been seen on television's "Midweek" and "Junior Bandbox" programs.[30]

It is just worth noting that the 'Python Lee' single was released under the band name of Libido. The *Billboard* article went on to give a good indication that Mooncrest, even if it was a 50/50 venture between B&C and Charisma, was very much a B&C company in its everyday make up and operations:

> With B&C supplying marketing services, Mooncrest will be run by a management committee comprising, in addition to Gopthal and Stratton Smith, Clive Crawley (label and promotion manager), formerly promotion manager for B&C–Charisma, Mike de Havilland, manager of the Mooncrest publishing subsidiary, and B&C directors, Jim Flynn and Fred Parsons. Hazel Griffiths has been named press officer ... Introduction of Mooncrest follows the development of B&C as a marketing company and the phasing out of the B&C and Peg labels. "The emphasis will be on quality pop singles as a means of breaking albums," commented Stratton Smith.[31]

Not mentioned in *Billboard* at the time – perhaps it was an emergent strategy ... or perhaps not – was that B&C and Peg label material was later to be reissued on Mooncrest:

> B&C Records has now completed the transfer of all product from the now–demised Pegasus label to Mooncrest. When Pegasus folded about a year ago, several titles were deleted and the rest scheduled to move over to Mooncrest.[32]

Mooncrest wasn't the only new label set up by B&C in 1973 – on the soul front, B&C started the People label. Most of the LPs released on People were licensed from the US Groove Merchant label and many singles were sourced from the Soul Dimension and Master Five labels, whilst other records came from labels such as Scepter and Shotgun.

At least one LP – by Doris Troy – was recorded specially for People in the UK. Webster Shrowder, who had started with Musicland and was now in charge of Trojan and Action, was put in charge of the label.

People was marketed as a 'black music' label, aligning itself with the current magazine of the same name, but much like B&C's other non-reggae labels there didn't seem to be any unifying strategy and music from straight–ahead soul, through light reggae to jazz–tinged R&B and even open jazz appeared on the label. A tape–only label compilation only managed to highlight the schitzophrenic nature of the label's offerings.

In August 1973, Tony Stratton Smith and Gail Colson left the rest of Charisma's staff at 70, Compton Street and moved in with B&C at 37, Soho Square, though communication problems soon forced the rest of Charisma's staff to follow. Coinciding with this move, B&C, as part of its recent transformation into a marketing company, started the process of getting a sales team on the road by advertising vacancies for sales staff, telephone sales staff, a marketing assistant and a general accounts clerk[33]. In the midst of this recruitment drive, B&C began an ambitious (not to say costly) television marketing campaign for the latest batch of records on Charisma and Mooncrest:

> B&C has launched a Summer Giants campaign involving eight albums which are being featured on television commercials this week and next in the Granada, ATV Midlands, Yorkshire, Tyne–Tees, Southern and Scotland areas. The albums featured are: Clifford T. Ward, Home Thoughts (CAS 1066); Lindisfarne Live (Class 2); Genesis Live (Class 1); Peter Hamill [sic], Chameleon In The Shadow Of The Night (CAS 1067); Alan Hull, Pipedream (CAS 1069); Capability Brown, Voice (CAS 1068); Nazareth, Razmanaz [sic] (CREST 1) and Music From Free Creek (CADS 101). The commercial uses music from Clifford T. Ward, Nazareth and Alan Hull [and promotion will] be backed up by music press colour advertising, window displays, posters and point of sale material.[34]

It was a couple more months before B&C's new sales recruits were trained up and their baptism by fire was in marketing *Charisma Disturbance*, a budget compilation put together to celebrate Charisma's fourth anniversary in November 1973. News of further collaboration between the B&C and Charisma camps came when *Music Week* reported on the creation of an international promotion department within what was now variously referred to in the music press as "B&C/Charisma", "Charisma/B&C" or any one of several variations thereof:

> An international promotion service department to back up Phonogram's marketing and distribution has been set up by B&C/Charisma Records. The department headed by Colin Richardson, previously with Charisma Artists, will aim at providing Phonogram with promotional material to back up that company's marketing and distribution of B&C and Charisma labels internationally – except for the USA and Canada. The new department is based at 37 Soho Square, London W.1., and Richardson, assisted by Bob Gilbert, previously with B&C sales, will be responsible for the coordination and dispatch of tapes, negatives and label copy.[35]

Although the two companies seemed to be 'cosying up' well, and despite discussions between Lee Gopthal and Tony Stratton Smith about a formal merger, this idea wasn't taken forward. By the tail end of 1973 the idea, probably much to Charisma's later relief, had been dropped with a – possibly erroneous – reason mooted by Stratton Smith to *Music Week*: "We finally decided against it because of administration problems and fears of muddying the waters. Both companies were successful and we didn't want to cramp the other's style."[36] Perhaps, tellingly, Charisma's Colin Richardson had the following to say about the relationship between Charisma and B&C:

> My recollection of Lee Gopthal is sketchy to say the least. I never really took to the guy and couldn't understand what Strat saw in him (other than finance–related) ... the B&C/Charisma relationship always seemed to me to be a bit of an odd pairing and one that was somewhat uneasy on the personnel side. A bit of 'them and us' ... though maybe that was just me.[37]

In spring 1974, a new artists and repertoire position was created within Mooncrest and, again, evidence that the label was more B&C than Charisma can be seen in the fact that the person chosen came from within B&C, which caused some further reshuffling of people and positions:

> Ian Mitchell is to take up a new position as [A&R] co–ordinator for Mooncrest Records after previously working as an accountant for the B&C Record Group. Matthew Williams has been appointed chief accountant to B&C Records, partly as a replacement and partly as a new position. He was previously accountant for Trojan Records.[38]

Mitchell soon moved again and in July was appointed managing director of B&C Music. At the same time, Clive Buckle, one of the sales team taken on in 1973, was made southern sales manager[39]

Also in 1974, B&C looked to further widen their share of the UK soul music market. This time, however, instead of licensing music from myriad labels as they did with Action and People, B&C set up to distribute product from the US Sussex label under that label's own imprint. Of the deal between B&C and Sussex, *Billboard* included brief details:

> B&C Records have completed a deal with U.S. label Sussex, previously with A&M Records for the U.K. First release is a batch of four Bill Withers' albums, and singles from Creative Source, Soul Searchers and Master Fleet. Deal was set up by B&C managing director Lee Gopthal and Sussex president Clarence Avant.[40]

The Sussex label remains a bit of an oddity in that the majority of the LPs issued by B&C still seemed to be available via A&M, their previous UK label. After B&C's demise, these albums were *still* listed in trade publications as being available from A&M. In an odd quirk of fate, perhaps, Sussex did not outlast B&C: Sussex's owner, Clarence Avant was raided and prosecuted by the US Internal Revenue Service for tax evasion, and the label closed in July 1975[41].

Meanwhile, to go back a bit, B&C, as already mentioned, seems to have moved people around the organisation with some regularity, and in October 1974, Steve Jukes, who had recently been put in charge of the Sussex label, took part in what looks suspiciously like a spot of job enlargement:

> As part of the restructuring and strengthening of its promotion activities the B&C/Charisma Group has created the new post of head of promotions. Steve Jukes who was recently appointed manager of the newly signed Sussex label will become head of the promotion department and Fraser Kennedy, who was previously area promotion manager for Scotland and the North East becomes field promotions manager. Changes have also been announced in the structure of the Mooncrest publishing company, which will now be jointly managed by Stephen Shane and Ian Warner ...[42]

Perhaps there were warning bells at Charisma that not all was well within the B&C group of companies. It might otherwise seem odd that, just as B&C was starting to expand, Stratton Smith started to think in terms of distancing Charisma from B&C. Toward the end of 1974 Stratton Smith is documented (admittedly in his own words and after B&C's subsequent liquidation) as having decided that it would be in Charisma's interests to curtail the long–term licensing deal with B&C:

> ... Stratton–Smith explained that he had made his intentions clear at Christmas that he would terminate Charisma's licensing deal with B&C as soon as alternative arrangements could be made. "A licensing deal was too limiting to allow Charisma to develop as I wanted,["] he said. Originally the deal with Phonogram had been planned to start in June but at B&C's request he had agreed to a three–month extension for catalogue sales "to give the company an opportunity to replace the lost business or to gear down to a reduced turnover."[43]

Ironically, it was success that brought about the end of B&C. Ken Boothe's rendition of Bread's *Everything I Own* was a major hit in the UK for Trojan in autumn 1974. B&C used Saga's pressing plant, perhaps because other manufacturers were starting to make noises about extended credit and monies owed them. Whatever the reason, as it turned out Trojan had difficulty in paying Saga the £20,000 pressing costs. Lee Gopthal had perhaps forgotten Island's strategy, in the mid–1960s, of licencing records that they expected to be big hits via a major label: Chris Blackwell, talking about this had said: "I'd seen independent labels die because they had a hit ... They'd run up a huge bill manufacturing the records and then they would have difficulty getting paid on time by retailers and they'd go bankrupt."[44] Perhaps Gopthal genuinely didn't realise that a company as large as B&C could be brought low by something as simple as cash flow problems. That or the size of the hit came as a complete surprise to the company.

Saga's owner, Marcel Rodd, was looking to expand and in March 1975, Saga advertised in *Music Week* to buy a record company as a going concern[45]. B&C, with its seemingly successful Mooncrest and Trojan labels and industry–rumoured cash flow problems, could easily fit the bill. What actually happened, whilst not illegal, remains perhaps morally questionable. Still, as they say, all's fair in business. Well, you've got to say something.

> ... [Saga's accountant, Bill] Ross telephoned B&C/Trojan [who] weren't prepared to sell but an agreement emerged between Rodd and B&C/Trojan's directors Lee Gopthal and Brian Gibbon[46] where, for a 10 per cent interest in the company, Saga would loan B&C [£150,000] to be secured on audited figures showing [£600,000] of net assets. The debenture was drawn up by Saga's solicitors. But meanwhile Bill Ross had spent a week in B&C/Trojan's accounts departments and brought back the

alarming news that the contract would have to be scrapped, as in his opinion, the company was "grossly in deficit" ... B&C/Trojan came back to Saga to say that provided Saga could conclude a deal within forty–eight hours they would sell the whole of the company for any figure, "provided it was not less than twenty–five–thousand pounds" ... That`s when Saga ... proposed the formation of new subsidiary companies, B&C Recordings Ltd and Trojan Recordings Ltd (with the board of directors identical to B&C Records Ltd and Trojan Records Ltd) and that on formation the new companies should have transferred to them the assets of the parent companies (the stock, recording contracts and masters) but not the liabilities (the growing mountain of unpaid bills) and that the new subsidiaries should then be immediately sold to Saga ... On the 31st May 1975, Saga handed over a cheque for just under [£30,000] to B&C/Trojan. But [instead] of using the cash to try and refloat their floundering company B&C/Trojan merely extinguished their bank overdraft ... then dismissed all their staff and applied to be put into voluntary liquidation.[47]

Notices of two creditors meetings, one for B&C Records Ltd. and one for Trojan Records Ltd., were posted in *The London Gazette* on 10th June, 1975[48]. These meetings were to take place at the Westbury Hotel, New Bond Street, Piccadilly, on 20th June, 1975, at 2.00 pm (for B&C) and 3.30 pm (for Trojan). A further pair of notices was placed in the same paper on 19th June regarding petitions brought by MCPS for the winding up of B&C and Trojan in the High Court of Chancery. The hearing was set for 7th July.

Goings on at B&C, in relation to Charisma's somewhat rushed deal with Phonogram, made the front page of *Music Week* but quite a lot was left unsaid:

> Charisma Records has signed a pressing and distribution deal with Phonogram for the UK and Eire. The pact coincides with news that B&C, which previously handled sales and distribution for Charisma is part of a takeover deal by Saga Records' parent company, Art and Sound Ltd (Saga Sound) ... All B&C employees, including those at the affiliated Trojan and Mooncrest publishing and recording companies, were given formal notice last Friday (Jun 6) but a rider clause said that some jobs would be saved by the Saga takeover. An announcement from Saga states: "Saga has purchased 100 percent of the shareholdings of B&C Recordings Ltd and Trojan Recordings Ltd, previously known as B&C Records and Trojan Records. Also included in this deal until August 31, this year, are our pressing rights to Charisma Records and thereafter unlimited selling rights on Charisma stocks on hand."[49]

It was a couple more weeks after the original news of the Saga takeover before *Music Week* announced B&C's liquidation, out of which several companies seem to have come out rather badly:

> The total estimated deficiency of Trojan Records and B&C Records, 300 people at a creditors' meeting at the Hanover Grand last Friday, were told, amounted to £594,453, with B&C accounting for £408,991 of the full amount. A statement of affairs relating to B&C showed book value assets of £355,972, of which £140,000 related to advance royalties, to an estimated realisable value of £116,000. MCPS with £31,350 was at the top

of the schedule of copyright creditors, followed by Carlin Music/Genesis (£23,665), Mooncrest Music (£17,094), Quarter (£14,795), B&C Music (£11,625) and Mountain/Carlin (£9,562). Among the unsecured creditors were Garrod and Lofthouse (£27,476), J. Upton (£24,243), E. J. Day (£11,263), CBS Manufacturing (£16,133), CRS (£11,473), National Publicity (£10,785) and Morgan Studios (£10,000). The total amounted to £316,932.26.[50]

In July 1975, Charisma moved out of 37, Soho Square and retrenched drastically to survive – further information is included in the sister publication, *The Famous Charisma Discography*. Once the crisis was over, Charisma expanded its staff base and brought in several ex–B&C staff, including Clive Crawley. Webster Shrowder, the managing director of Trojan and head of the People and Action labels, was taken on by Saga but left to form Vulcan Records along with Junior Lincoln[51], who had run a resurrected version of the Ashanti label for B&C. Under Saga's ownership, the B&C, Mooncrest and Trojan labels were reactivated, and still exist today, though now several changes of ownership later.

Lee Gopthal, Webster Shrowder, Joe Sinclair and Desmond Bryan were listed as directors of Muzik City Record Shops Ltd. as at 1975, but on 22nd January, 1976, the company went into voluntary winding up, with things dragging on until the final creditors' meeting on 1st December, 1978[52]. It is unclear whether Gopthal was still involved to any extent with Musicland Record Stores Ltd., but this company too was dissolved on 14th February, 1977[53]. Lee Gopthal, following a certain amount of silence, was next reported in the trade press as head of A&R for RCA UK[54]. After this, he moved away from the music industry and went into commerce, type unspecified. He died on 29 August 1997.

Tony Stratton Smith spoke to *Music Week*[55] saying that the reason behind B&C's demise was that they had introduced a sales force despite not having a large enough product base to make this sales expansion viable. Added to this, he said, was a bad sales performance in the first three months of 1975. However, perhaps B&C's demise was due to more deep–seated reasons. Neither B&C nor Trojan, unlike Charisma, were particularly concerned with artist development, probably because the business model was that of licensing existing product from various sources. Consequently, the emphasis tended to be on singles and budget compilation LPs rather than on more lucrative full price album sales. By focusing on singles and budget albums, margin on a per unit basis would never be anything but fairly low. Charisma survived where B&C failed because Stratton Smith was interested, first and foremost, in signing artists whose careers he could develop. More importantly, he concentrated on 'album artists'. Hit singles were lucrative in the short term but worked best as promotional tools for albums. The only sustained success that B&C had with full price album product was with Mooncrest – but Mooncrest's best-selling albums were licensed from production companies, such as Mountain and Sandy Roberton's September Productions[56]. The last word sits with Rob Bell and, as last words go, it speaks volumes about B&C:

> There was no quality control at all, really. I don't think ... Lee [Gopthal] had a huge amount of artistic appreciation. The majority of the folks involved saw the whole thing merely as a business, which of course it was.[57]

The B&C Discography: 1968 to 1975

Section sources

1. Public Record Office Catalogue Reference PRO/BT26/1237/9410. Accessed from http://www.movinghere.org.uk/deliveryfiles/PRO/BT26_1237_9410/0/1.pdf (05/08/2012).
2. According to De Koningh, M. & Cane–Honeycott, L. (in *Young Gifted and Black*, 2003, Sanctuary, p. 29) Beat and Commercial Records Ltd. was set up by Lee Gopthal and Tony Stratton Smith. This is perfectly possible but, if so, it is odd that Stratton Smith's name does not crop up again in official documentation until 1969.
3. De Koningh, M. & Cane–Honeycott, L. (in *Young Gifted and Black*, 2003, Sanctuary, p. 42) note that there is anecdotal evidence of a branch of Musicland existing as early as 1965, but could find no corroborative documentary evidence.
4. Bell, R. (25/03/2009) *Joy, Tears & Endless Kicks – My Life In Music, Part 4*. Accessed from: http://www.sequelmusic.com/index.php?l1=1&articleID=158&page= (10/03/2012).
5. HR Taylor did not start distributing Trojan until around June 1970: the original article also mentions the Muzik City chain of record shops, which were started in 1971, so this quote includes various memories spanning 1968 to 1971.
6. Bell, R. (30/03/2009) *Joy, Tears & Endless Kicks – My Life In Music, Part 5*. Accessed from: http://www.sequelmusic.com/index.php?l1=1&articleID=301&page= (10/03/2012).
7. Advert (12/05/1968) Spotlight On London. *Billboard*.
8. Blackwell, C., quoted in *Island History* (no author or publication date attributed). Accessed from: http://www.islandrecords.co.uk/history.php (09/04/2012)
9. Trojan was originally set up in 1967 as an Island subsidiary label, but became dormant in early 1968 after the release of TR 015. The B&C/Island joint venture started later in 1968 with TR 600.
10. B&C was also, to a currently unknown extent, associated with Libra Music and Pinewalk Music.
11. No author attributed (13/11/1971) Spotlight On London: The Vigorous, Resourceful Independents. *Billboard*.
12. Palmer, P. (12/04/1969) International New Reports: London. *Billboard*.
13. As regards addresses, the first fifteen or so Island singles included a 4, Rutland Gate Mews, SW7 address. After a few months with no address listed, both singles and LPs, including Island's highly successful series of risqué LPs on the Surprise label, included the 108 Cambridge Road address. By 1968 Island started to use a rather more upmarket 155–157 Oxford Street address on LP sleeves. Action label LPs (and the various reggae labels) used the Music House address – ACLP 6004 includes the following: "A member of B & C Group Music House 12 Neasden Lane London Tel 01 – 459 5222." All B&C, Charisma and Mooncrest LPs included the 37 Soho Square address.
14. No author attributed (17/11/1973) Charisma – artist's label, *Music Week*.
15. Email dated 13th November 2009.
16. Photograph of letter included in the booklet accompanying *The Famous Charisma Box* 4–CD set (CASBOX 1, 1993).
17. No author attributed (13/06/1970) International News Reports: Island Distrib Tie on Trojan, *Billboard*.
18. No author attributed (13/11/1971) Spotlight On London: West Indian Population Sparks New UK Music Trend, *Billboard*.
19. Palaree, P. (20/05/1972) International News Reports: From The Music Capitals of the World: London, *Billboard*.
20. No author attributed (27/03/1971) International News Reports: From The Music Capitals of the World: Reggae Outlet Forms Label, *Billboard*.
21. Notice of release of B&C label 8–tracks and cassettes (of previously–released BCM series LPs) was still being documented in trade publications as late as February 1973, which smacks somewhat of B&C acting as a record label very shortly in advance of its supposed successor, Mooncrest, being launched. It's difficult to disentangle and one gets the distinct impression that B&C was making it up as it went along and claiming some sort of strategy after the event when talking to the press.
22. EMI had taken over from Island/Philips/Phondisc, though EMI would later set up joint distribution with Island and all B&C–related product was listed in trade publications from around mid–1973 as being distributed by Island/EMI.
23. No author attributed (28/10/1972) International News Reports: Island, B&C Split With Trojan Label, *Billboard*.
24. These labels were later augmented, however. In 1973 B&C/Trojan started a new version of the Ashanti label, run by Junior Lincoln. Lincoln had previously run Ashanti as a sub–label of his own Bamboo label, which had been a rival to Trojan until Bamboo went bust. In 1974 Mooncrest (rather than Trojan) picked up the licence for the Dragon label from Island – labels included the text, "Manufactured by Mooncrest Records Ltd", though this was later changed to the more usual, "Marketed by B&C Records".

25. Palmer, P. (29/07/1972) International News Reports: From The Music Capitals of the World: London, *Billboard*.
26. Mike de Havilland (correct spelling) had recently changed his name from Mike Paice.
27. No author attributed (01/12/1973) Mooncrest sub–deal, *Music Week*.
28. Mooncrest was referred to as a "heavy rock" label in Japan: see Eguchi, H. (08/09/1973) International News: From the Music Capitals of the World: Tokyo, *Billboard*. The article also referred to the label having been set up in May 1972, which presumably relates to the setting up of the Mooncrest Music publishing company and not the record label. It is comforting to know that, even at the time, journalists had difficulty keeping up with B&C–related companies.
29. A and A North had also previously been signed to B&C, whilst Richie Francis had been signed to Pegasus.
30. No author attributed (10/03/1973) International News Reports: B&C–Charisma Label Widens Cos' Base, *Billboard*.
31. Ibid.
32. Bromeu, J. (01/06/1974) International News: From the Music Capitals of the World: London, *Billboard*.
33. No author attributed (11/08/1973) Advert, *Music Week*.
34. No author attributed (08/09/1973) B&C plans 'Summer' tele–push, *Music Week*.
35. No author attributed (01/09/1973) B&C–Charisma set up promo dept, *Music Week*.
36. No author attributed (17/11/1973) Charisma – artist's label, *Music Week*.
37. Email dated 11/03/2012.
38. No author attributed (20/04/1974) International: International Turntable, *Billboard*.
39. No author attributed (27/07/1974) International: International Turntable, *Billboard*.
40. Jones, P. (29/09/1974) International: From the Music Capitals of the World: London, *Billboard*.
41. After its offices were padlocked by the IRS.
42. White, C. (05/10/1974) International News: From the Music Capitals of the World: London, *Billboard*.
43. No author attributed (05/07/1975) Charisma surges back with new talent push, *Music Week*.
44. Blackwell, C., quoted in *Island History* (no author or publication date attributed). Accessed from: http://www.islandrecords.co.uk/history.php (09/04/2012)
45. No author attributed (10/1976) Reggae Business, *Black Music Magazine*. p23
46. Brian Gibbon almost immediately joined Charisma as deputy managing director. Or was already working for both B&C and Charisma.
47. No author attributed (10/1976) Reggae Business, *Black Music Magazine*. pp23-4
48. De Koningh, M. & Cane–Honeycott, L. (2003) *Young Gifted and Black*. Sanctuary, p. 76.
49. Jones, P. (14/06/1975) Charisma to Phonogram as Saga acquires B&C, *Music Week*.
50. No author attributed (28/06/1975) Trojan–B&C liquidation, *Music Week*.
51. No author attributed (13/09/1975) International: Trojan Execs Form a label, *Billboard*. The company was originally going to be called Viking Records and is named as such in this article.
52. De Koningh, M. & Cane–Honeycott, L. (2003) *Young Gifted and Black*. Sanctuary, pp. 30–31.
53. Ibid.
54. Jones, P. (25/12/1976) International: From The Music Capitals of the World: London, *Billboard*.
55. No author attributed (05/07/1975) Charisma surges back with new talent push, *Music Week*.
56. Sadly, for Saga, both license deals had come to an end immediately prior to Saga acquiring Mooncrest. Mountain quickly turned itself into a record label, with distribution by Phonogram, and successfully reissued the entire Nazareth album back catalogue. Sandy Roberton continued to license his records to the resurrected Mooncrest.
57. De Koningh, M. & Cane–Honeycott, L. (2003) *Young Gifted and Black*. Sanctuary, p. 47.

Michael de Koningh and Laurence Cane–Honeysett's *Young Gifted and Black: The Story of Trojan Records* (Sanctuary, 2003) is highly recommended for further information on Lee Gopthal and B&C. Although focused on the Trojan series of labels it provides a great deal of contextualisation of material in the organisational history in this discography.

Introduction to the discographies

Label designs

The listings only include original label design information where one or more records in a particular catalogue sequence appeared on more than one design. Records on Stable, Mooncrest, Sussex, People and Seven Sun only appeared on one label design, as did LPs on Action's ACLP/ACLS sequence, so label information is not required for these.

7" label designs	LP label designs
AC1 – Action: orange and yellow	BC1 – B&C: black with silver logo
AC2 – Action: black with green logo	BC2 – B&C: black with large green logo
AC3 – Action: light grey with blue logo	BC3 – B&C: black with small green logo
AC4 – Action: 'blue singer' logo	CH1 – Charisma: scroll, no B&C credit
BC1 – B&C: black with silver logo	CH2 – Charisma: scroll, B&C credit
BC2 – B&C: black with green logo	PE1 – Pegasus: flying horse
CH1 – Charisma: scroll, no B&C credit	PE2 – Peg: clothes peg
CH2 – Charisma: scroll, B&C credit	
PE1 – Pegasus: flying horse	
PE2 – Peg: clothes peg	

Pressing companies used by B&C

The majority of early releases were pressed by Orlake at their Dagenham plant. These have rough-textured labels and matrix numbers in the run-off have "+" between each component, e.g. "CB+100+A". The B&C group of companies also used Philips, whose 7" singles are easily distinguished by three-pronged die-cut centres or large centre holes (Orlake singles have either four-pronged die-cut or solid centres). On Philips pressings, the matrix numbers in the run-off include a double forward slash, such as "CB 122 A//1".

In 1970 B&C switched from Philips/Orlake to EMI. EMI pressings are distinguished by the inclusion of "U" at the end of the run-off matrix number, e.g. "CB 130 A–1U": this indicates EMI pressings for non-EMI companies. The first EMI-pressed single in the CB sequence looks to be CB 129, dating the switch at around August 1970, which looks to be confirmed by September 1970 CAS LP releases being EMI pressings. Although the original pressings of CAS 1018 to CAS 1022 were by EMI, the 7" singles pressed up to promote the LPs, were Orlake pressings – perhaps Orlake was more reasonably priced when it came to small pressing runs.

By late 1974 it looks as though B&C was using any pressing company that would extend it credit. In November 1974, at least some new records and back catalogue repressings on Mooncrest look like Lyntone pressings, whilst Saga and CBS were also used. It is very difficult to unearth quite what was happening toward the end – obviously, B&C tried to keep its cashflow problems secret, but because it did this semi-successfully speculation is rife, whilst hard facts are somewhat thin on the ground. Certainly, over £16,000 was owed to CBS Manufacturing when B&C was wound up.

Sources used in lists

[1] *The New Records* – monthly publication
[2] *New Cassettes & Cartridges* – monthly publication
[3] *The New Singles* – weekly publication
[4] *Music Master* 2nd edition (1976)
[5] *Music Master* 5th edition (1979)
[6] *The Famous Charisma Box – The History of Charisma Records 1968–1985* – booklet from 4–CD boxed set (1993) (yes, EMI got the 25th anniversary wrong)
[7] *Charisma & Pre Complete British Singles: 1970–1984 / B&C Complete British Singles: 1969–1980 / Mooncrest Complete British Singles: 1973–1978 / Pegasus/Peg Complete British Singles: 1971–1972* – compiled, in a ring–bound booklet with listings for other labels, published privately by Paul Pelletier (1995)
[8] Promotional record labels
[9] *Budget Price Records* – quarterly publication
[10] *Cassettes & Cartridges* – monthly publication
[11] *Gramophone Popular Record Catalogue* – quarterly publication

The first three sources above, along with *Budget Price Records*, were published by Francis Antony, whilst the *Music Master* series was published by John Humphries. *Gramophone* and *Cassettes & Cartridges* were published by General Gramophone Publications (the latter, coincidentally, printed by the E.J. Day Group, which also printed many B&C Group record sleeves and ended up being owed over £62,000 when B&C went under). Each source is represented in the listings by superscript numbers: e.g. [1] next to a list item represents that the information was sourced from *The New Records*.

Release and deletion dates

Release dates are sourced, where possible, from contemporary trade publications, *The New Records* and *The New Cassettes and Cartridges*, which were issued monthly, and *The New Singles*, which was issued weekly. The British Library's holdings were used, though many issues are missing. Some gaps were filled from other collections, but it has proven impossible to gain access to thirty or so missing issues. The 1976 *Music Master 2nd Edition* was used to source release dates for LPs only, whilst the *5th Edition* includes listings of all formats, including tape versions. Quarterly publications, *Budget Price Records* and *Gramophone* were used as a last resort, though *Gramophone*'s monthly magazine, *Cassettes and Cartridges*, helped fill a few eleventh hour gaps.

Dates sourced from *The New Records* and *The New Cassettes and Cartridges* often tends to be a month out because both were issued mid–month. For example, an April release notified in March would miss the April edition if that issue had already gone to print. The listing, therefore, would appear in the May edition, itself issued mid–April. Wherever there is a discrepancy in release date, all conflicting sources are listed. Where there is no conflict between different sources, only *The New Records* or *The New Cassettes and Cartridges* is shown as source. Where the release date for singles indicates two possible dates a week apart this means that the specific edition and one or more follow–up editions of *The New Singles* were not available during research. *The New Singles* lists releases from the previous fortnight, so depending on whether (and which) subsequent issues are missing you can; a) pinpoint the exact week; b) be left with a two week window; c) have no clue whatsoever if four consecutive editions are missing (which they often are). Where no information was available Paul Pelletier's listings were used. Pelletier's sources comprised *The New Singles*, *Records of the Month*, *Pop Singles*, *Music Week* and the BBC Gramophone Library's record purchasing accounts. Many dates are sourced from promotional copies of the records. There are some interesting mismatches along the way – make of these what you will.

Deletion dates are taken from *Music Master 2nd Edition*, which includes dates for LP deletions advised between 1973 and the end of 1975 and *Music Master 5th Edition*, which includes all deletions advised up to the end of 1978. However, it is worth noting that in *Music Master 2nd Edition* all B&C deletions are listed as March 1974: the whole thing has a look of 'tidying up' about it and so these dates are probably not entirely accurate.

The B&C group started to issue tapes in 1972 and release (and occasional deletion) dates are included for both cassettes and 8–track cartridges. Where the listings state that no tape versions were notified to trade publications it is still just possible that one or two of these albums were issued in these formats. Toward the end of 1974 and early 1975 it looks as though B&C was cherry–picking which LPs to also release on tape – probably based on which were likely to bring in cash sharpish. A combination of needing money quickly and of mounting unpaid bills with suppliers probably didn't help matters.

There are one or two potentially confusing issues when it comes to tape releases. Firstly, B&C label CAS series LPs had their tape versions released on the Peg label, to which B&C artists had been transferred the previous year (well, Pegasus to be exact, but this had already metamorphosed into Peg). Secondly, when Pegasus/Peg label LPs were reissued on Mooncrest, tape versions were not reissued simply because there were very large stocks of original Pegasus/Peg tapes still available.

Existing stocks of B&C–era tapes became available via the resurrected Mooncrest/B&C/Trojan as from 1976. 8–tracks still remaining on catalogue were deleted when this format ceased to be commercially available in the UK (probably 1979). In fact, many still–sealed 8–track versions crop up on eBay. If no–one else ultimately did well out of B&C, it looks like Precision Tapes did – they certainly didn't end up as one of B&C's many creditors!

Recommended retail price

Prices for LPs and tapes are sourced from *The New Records*, *The New Cassettes and Cartridges* and the *Music Master* publications. Generally, the prices shown in *The New Records* and *The New Cassettes and Cartridges* are correct and so these are used as the main source. *Music Master* prices are shown where no other price source was available or where the price differs from that shown in *The New Records* and so on.

Where there is only the difference of 1p in stated RRP in different sources – e.g. £2.14 as against £2.15 for LPs – I haven't bothered to document this. Just bear in mind that wherever *The New Records* states £2.15, *Music Master*, if it includes a price, says £2.14 fairly consistently. Adding this discrepancy in each individual case made for some very messy listings but didn't really add much value, hence the decision not to document except here. However, a 4p discrepancy is a different matter –I mean, that's almost a Shilling!

Discographies

Labels are listed in the order in which they first released records. Therefore, the listings begin with the Action label (first release 1968) and finish with the Seven Sun label (first B&C–related release scheduled for June 1975). LP catalogue sequences are listed first, followed by 7" catalogue sequences and promotional records, irrespective of whether the first issue on any particular label was an LP or single: this is done purely to provide the book with a less chaotic structure. The labels covered are, in order of appearance: Action; Stable; B&C/Charisma; Pegasus/Peg; Mooncrest; People; Dragon; Sussex; Seven Sun. Dragon is included because, although a reggae label, it was a sub–label of Mooncrest, rather than of Trojan (Trojan and related labels are not covered). These listings are not concerned with records released after B&C's liquidation so do not include subsequent Mooncrest or B&C label releases issued by the relaunched B&C Recordings Ltd.

Just to confuse the issue B&C shared its main CAS and CB sequences with Charisma. Therefore Charisma's CAS and CB releases are shown alongside B&C's up until the point at which B&C ceased releasing records on each sequence: this is some nebulous point near the end of 1971 (officially) or start of 1972 (probably) for CAS sequence LPs and August 1972 for CB sequence singles. Full listings of all Charisma catalogue sequences issued during its association with B&C are available in *The Famous Charisma Discography*, an earlier publication in the acclaimed *Famous British Record Labels* series.

Action

Releases for the Action label were chosen by John Abbey, a noted blues and soul expert, and as far as cherry–picking goes, the original incarnation of the label takes some beating. Almost every record is a classic, and collectors are well aware that the records do not come cheaply. The label petered out in late 1970, which would seem to coincide with Abbey starting the Contempo label, along with the like–minded Bob Kilborn. Contempo followed the same model as Action – Abbey and Kilborn licensed music from the US Roker, Canyon, Soul Clock and RRG labels, but for release via Polydor's new Mojo imprint rather than via B&C or Action. The Action label was revived in 1971 but whether Abbey was still involved is unlikely and, again, the label petered out in mid–1972. It was revived yet again in mid–1973, but in 1974 became dormant again – perhaps because Action artists were now being licensed to the newer (and rather more 'hip') People label. Its final revival was in 1975, this time as an 'ethnic' reggae outlet.

Issues from 1968 to 1970 included information on the label as to which US label had licensed the tracks to B&C: when the label was revived in 1971, very few records followed this example.

ACLP/ACLS sequence LPs

All LPs in this sequence were on the orange/yellow label design. All bar the Z.Z. Hill, Al Greene and Jimmy Reed LPs were issued in mono. Only the Z.Z. Hill album is listed with both stereo and mono versions[1], though the 1970 B&C/Action/Stable catalogue lists stereo releases only for all three. All Action LPs were listed as available in the 1970 catalogue but all had been deleted by 1974[4].

The B&C Discography: 1968 to 1975

ACLP 6001   **THE FANTASTIC JOHNNY 'C': Boogaloo Down Broadway**

1. Boogaloo Down Broadway
2. Cool Broadway
3. Barefootin'
4. The Bounce
5. Land Of 1,000 Dances
6. Shout Bamalama

1. Got What You Need
2. Baby I Need You
3. (She's) Some Kind Of Wonderful
4. Stand By Me
5. New Love
6. Warm And Tender Love

Rel: 1968 or 1969
RRP: not advised

ACLP 6002   **BARBARA MASON: Oh How It Hurts**

1. Oh How It Hurts
2. Poor Girl In Trouble
3. I Need Love
4. You Can Depend On Me
5. I Do Love You
6. Game Of Love

1. Yes, I'm Ready
2. If You Don't
3. Is It Me
4. Forever
5. I Don't Want To Lose You
6. For Your Love

Rel: 1968 or 1969
RRP: not advised

ACLP 6003   **BRENDA AND THE TABULATIONS: Dry Your Eyes**

1. Dry Your Eyes
2. Walk On By
3. God Only Knows
4. Who's Loving You
5. Summertime
6. Where Did Our Love Go

1. Just Once In A Lifetime
2. Forever
3. Stay Together Young Lovers
4. Hey Boy
5. Oh Lord What Are You Doing To Me
6. The Wash

Rel: 1969
RRP: not advised

ACLP/ACLS 6004   **Z.Z. HILL: Whole Lot Of Soul (MONO/STEREO)**

1. When Something Is Wrong With My Baby
2. What Am I Living For
3. Nothing Takes The Place Of You
4. Knock On Wood
5. Steal Away
6. You Gonna Make Me Cry

1. You Send Me
2. Midnight Hour
3. When A Man Loves A Woman
4. Make Me Yours
5. Nothing Can Change The Love I Have For You
6. Greatest Love

Rel: Mar 1969[1]
RRP: 37/5[1]

Although both mono and stereo versions are listed in The New Records, there doesn't otherwise seem to be corroboration of a mono version existing.

ACLP 6005   **VARIOUS ARTISTS: Action Packed Soul Volume 1**

1. Competition Ain't Nothing (Carl Carlton)
2. Please (Joe Hinton)
3. Sockin' 1–2–3–4 (John Roberts)
4. It's All Over Now (Clarence Carter And Calvin Thomas)
5. Mr Soul (Bud Harper)
6. Tell Him No (The Bell Brothers)
7. No Cure For The Blues (The Lamp Sisters)
8. Spicks and Specks (Bobby Day)

1. Dancin' Man (Ernie K Doe)
2. Share Your Love With Me (Bobby Bland)
3. Something's Got A Hold On Me (Jeanette Williams)
4. That's All A Part Of Loving You (Al 'TNT' Braggs)
5. Baby I Need Your Love (Bobby Williams)
6. Heartaches, Heartaches (O.V. Wright)
7. You're Almost Tuff (Roy Head)
8. Grab Your Clothes (Minnie Epperson)

Rel: Apr 1969[1]
RRP: 37/5[1]

ACLP 6006   **BOBBY BLAND: A Piece Of Gold**

1. Back In The Same Old Bag
2. Shae Your Love With Me
3. Poverty
4. If You Could Read My Mind
5. Dust Got In Daddy's Eyes
6. These Hands

1. Piece Of Gold
2. Save Your Love For Me
3. Who Will The Next Fool Be
4. Good Time Charlie
5. How Does A Cheating Woman Feel
6. Yield Not To Temptation

Rel: Mar 1969[1]
RRP: 37/5[1]

The B&C Discography: 1968 to 1975

ACLP 6007   BETTY HARRIS: Soul Perfection
1. Ride Your Pony
2. What A Sad Feeling
3. Bad Luck
4. I'm Gonna Git Ya
5. Show It
6. Can't Last Much Longer
7. I Don't Wanna Hear It
8. Sometime

1. Mean Man
2. Lonely Hearts
3. Hook Line N Sinker
4. What'd I Do Wrong
5. Trouble With My Lover
6. Nearer To You
7. I'm Evil Tonight
8. 12 Red Roses

Rel: May 1969[1]
RRP: 37/5[1]

ACLS 6008   AL GREENE: Back Up Train (STEREO)
1. Back Up Train
2. Hot Wire
3. Stop And Check Myself
4. Let Me Help You
5. I'm Reachin' Out
6. Don't Hurt Me No More

1. Lovers Hideaway
2. Don't Leave Me
3. What's It All About
4. I'll Be Good To You
5. Guilty
6. That's All It Takes (Lady)
7. Get Yourself Together

Rel: Jun/Jul '69[1]
RRP: 37/5[1]

ACLP 6009   VARIOUS ARTISTS: These Kind Of Blues Volume One
1. Tennessee Woman (Fention Robinson)
2. Little Boy Blue (Bobby Bland)
3. Okie Dokie Stomp (Clarence "Gatemouth" Brown)
4. Texas Flood (Larry Davis)
5. Hound Dog (Willie Mae Thornton)
6. Pledging My love (Johnny Ace)
7. You Got Money (Clarence "Gatemouth" Brown)
8. These Kind Of Blues Pt 1 (Junior Parker)

1. These Kind Of Blues Pt 2 (Junior Parker)
2. She's Gone (Jimmy McCracklin)
3. You've Got To Pass This Way Again (Fention Robinson)
4. Bobby's Blues (Bobby Bland)
5. Just Before Dawn (Clarence "Gatemouth" Brown)
6. That's Alright (Junior Parker)
7. Keep On Doggin' (Roscoe Gordon)
8. Stormy Monday Blues (Bobby Bland)

Rel: Oct 1969[1]
RRP: 37/5[1]

ACLP 6010   GENE CHANDLER: Live On Stage
1. Rainbow '65
2. If You Can't Be True
3. Soul Hootenanny
4. Monkey Time
5. What Now

1. Just Be True
2. Ain't No Use
3. Bless Our Love
4. A Song Called Soul

Rel: Jul 1969[1]
RRP: 37/5[1]

Side 1 label includes the credit "Introduction – Pervis Spann" and side 2 label includes the credit "Introduction – E. Rodney Jones". This was originally issued on the US Constellation label in 1965 as *Live On Stage In '65*.

ACLS 6011   JIMMY REED: Down In Virginia (STEREO)
1. Sugar Sugar Woman
2. Don't Light My Fire
3. Slow Walking Mama
4. Jump And Shout
5. Down In Virginia

1. Check Yourself
2. I Shot An Arrow To The Sky
3. Ghetto Woman Blues
4. Big Boss Lady
5. I Need You So
6. The Judge Should Know.

Rel: Oct 1969[1]
RRP: 37/5[1]

Insert. The front sleeve includes a stereo credit on all copies viewed during research. However, stereo copies are known to have "ACLP" (mono) matrix numbers in the run-off. This may just be because B&C didn't usually bother to give different catalogue prefixes to stereo records. In fact this Action LP sequence seems to be the only sequence where a distinction was made – on labels and sleeves at any rate, if not in matrix numbers.

ACMP sequence LP

Despite the Action label logo on the sleeve, the labels were of the current B&C black/green design. Action ceased releasing records in early 1970 and was restarted in late 1971. The following LP was the only LP release from Action's second wave of releases and was the last LP issued on the label, which concentrated thereafter on singles.

ACMP 100 EDDIE 'GUITAR' BURNS: Bottle Up And Go
1. She's In L.A
2. Bottle Up And Go
3. Cross Your Heart
4. Detroit Women (Lookey Here Babe)
5. Bad Bad Whisky

1. Kansas City
2. Whisky Headed Woman
3. Your Daddy Ain't Foolin'
4. Vicksburg Blues
5. I Call It Love

Label: BC3
Rel: Oct 1972[1]
RRP: £1.42[4]
£2.25[1]

ACT 4500 sequence 7" singles

The 1970 B&C/Action/Stable catalogue lists all releases up to ACT 4553 as being still on catalogue, except for ACT 4521, which was listed as not issued. One or two records released on the first label design are confirmed as also existing on the second label design. Given that all first label design records were available in 1970, more than those confirmed may exist on the second label design.

ACT 4500 WILMER AND THE DUKES: Give Me One More Chance / Get It
Label: AC1   Rel: 20 Sep 1968[3]

ACT 4501 LITTLE CARL CARLTON: Competion Ain't Nothing / Three Way Love
Label: AC1   Rel: 20 Sep 1968[3]

ACT 4502 ERNIE K. DOE: Dancing Man / Later For Tomorrow
Label: AC1   Rel: 20 Sep 1968[3]

ACT 4503 MINNIE EPPERSON: Grab Your Clothes (And Get On Out) / No Love At All
Label: AC1   Rel: 20 Sep 1968[3]

ACT 4504 BUDDY ACE: Got To Get Myself Together / Darling Depend On Me
Label: AC1   Rel: 4 Oct 1968[3]

ACT 4505 O.V. WRIGHT: Oh Baby Mine / Working Your Game
Label: AC1   Rel: 4 Oct 1968[3]

ACT 4506 AL "TNT" BRAGGS: Earthquake / How Long (Do You Hold On)
Label: AC1   Rel: 4 Oct 1968[3]
Four-prong die-cut cente copies have the usual orange colour labels, whilst solid centred copies have a distinct red colour to the labels.

ACT 4507 HARMONICA FATS: Tore Up / I Get So Tired
Label: AC1   Rel: 15 Nov 1968[3]

ACT 4508 VERNON GARRETT: Shine It On / Things Are Looking Better
Label: AC1   Rel: 25 Oct 1968[3]

The B&C Discography: 1968 to 1975

ACT 4509 — **BOBBY WILLIAMS: Baby I Need Your Love / Try It Again**
Label: AC1   **Rel:** 15 Nov 1968[3]

ACT 4510 — **THE BELL BROTHERS: Tell Him No / Throw Away The Key**
Label: AC1   **Rel:** 15 Nov 1968[3]

ACT 4511 — **JOHN ROBERTS: I'll Forget You / Be My Baby**
Label: AC1   **Rel:** unknown

ACT 4512 — **ERNIE K–DOE: Gotta Pack My Bags / How Sweet You Are**
Label: AC1   **Rel:** unknown

ACT 4513 — **THE BROTHERS TWO: Here I Am In Love Again / I'm Tired Of You Baby**
Label: AC1   **Rel:** 6 Dec 1968[3]

ACT 4514 — **LITTLE CARL CARLTON: 46 Drums, 1 Guitar / Why Don't They Leave Us Alone**
Label: AC1   **Rel:** 6 Dec 1968[3]

ACT 4515 — **ROOSEVELT GRIER: People Make The World / Hard To Forget**
Label: AC1   **Rel:** 6 Dec 1968[3]

ACT 4516 — **RUBAIYATS: Omar Khayyam / Tomorrow**
Label: AC1   **Rel:** unknown

ACT 4517 — **CHUCK TROIS AND THE AMAZING MAZE: Call On You / The Woodsman**
Label: AC1   **Rel:** unknown

ACT 4518 — **ROY LEE JOHNSON: So Anna You Love Me / ROY LEE JOHNSON AND HIS BAND: Boogaloo No. 3 (Instrumental)**
Label: AC1   **Rel:** 24 Jan 1969[3]

ACT 4519 — **EDDIE BUSTER FOREHAND: Young Boy Blues / You Were Meant For Me**
Label: AC1   **Rel:** 17 Jan 1969[3]
B–side title not confirmed – of the two variations listed in various places this sounds most likely.

ACT 4520 — **ALICE CLARK: You Got A Deal / Say You'll Never Leave Me**
Label: AC1   **Rel:** 7 Mar 1969[3]

ACT 4521 — **NO RELEASE**
The B&C/Action/Stable catalogue for 1970 confirms no release on this catalogue number.

ACT 4522 — **DEE DEE SHARP: What Kind Of Lady / You're Gonna Miss Me (When I'm Gone)**
Label: AC1   **Rel:** 14 Feb 1969[3]

ACT 4523 — **THE INTRUDERS: Slow Drag / So Glad I'm Yours**
Label: AC1   **Rel:** 10 Jan 1969[3]

The B&C Discography: 1968 to 1975

ACT 4524   BOBBY BLAND: Rockin' In The Same Old Boat / Wouldn't You Rather Have Me?
Label: AC1   **Rel:** 10 Jan 1969[3]

ACT 4525   DELLA HUMPHREY: Don't Make The Good Girls Go Bad / Your Love Is All I Need
Label: AC1   **Rel:** 24 Jan 1969[3]

ACT 4526   AL "TNT" BRAGGS: I'm A Good Man/I Like What You Do To Me
Label: AC1   **Rel:** 7 Mar 1969[3]

ACT 4527   O.V. WRIGHT: I Want Everyone To Know / I'm Gonna Forget About You
Label: AC1   **Rel:** 7 Mar 1969[3]

ACT 4528   LITTLE RICHARD AND HIS BAND: Baby What You Want Me To Do (Pt. 1) / Baby What You Want Me To Do (Pt. 2)
Label: AC1   **Rel:** 14 Feb 1969[3]

ACT 4529   NORMAN JOHNSON AND THE SHOWMEN: You're Everything / Our Love Will Grow
Label: AC1   **Rel:** unknown

ACT 4530   THE PRIME MATES: Hot Tamales (Part 1) / Hot Tamales (Part 2)
Label: AC1   **Rel:** unknown

ACT 4531   MELVIN DAVIS: Save It (Never Too Late) / This Love Was Meant To Be
Label: AC1   **Rel:** 2 May 1969[3]

ACT 4532   Z.Z. HILL: Make Me Yours / What Am I Living For?
Label: AC1   **Rel:** unknown

ACT 4533   BOBBY MARCHAN: Ain't No Reason For Girls To Be Lonely / Ain't No Reason For Girls To Be Lonely (Instrumental)
Label: AC1   **Rel:** 2 May 1969[3]

ACT 4534   JEANETTE WILLIAMS: Stuff / You Gotta Come Through
Label: AC1   **Rel:** 23 May 1969[3]

ACT 4535   BETTY HARRIS: Ride Your Pony / Trouble With My Lover
Label: AC1   **Rel:** 17 May 1969[3]

ACT 4536   EDDIE WILSON: Shing–A–Ling Stroll [see below] / Don't Kick The Teenager Around
Label: AC1   **Rel:** 13 June or 20 June 1969[3]
Early labels are incorrectly credited as "Shing–A–King Stroll".

ACT 4537   CARL CARLTON: Look At Mary Wonder / Bad For Each Other
Label: AC1   **Rel:** 13 June or 20 June 1969[3]

ACT 4538   BOBBY BLAND: Gotta Get To Know You / Baby I'm On My Way
Label: AC1   **Rel:** 13 June or 20 June 1969[3]

The B&C Discography: 1968 to 1975

ACT 4539 THE OLYMPICS: Baby Do The Philly Dog / Mine Exclusively
Label: AC1   Rel: 27 Jun 1969[3]

ACT 4540 AL GREENE: Don't Hurt Me No More / Get Yourself Together
Label: AC1   Rel: 18 Jul 1969[3]

ACT 4541 BRENDA AND THE TABULATIONS: That's In The Past / I Can't Get Over You
Label: AC1   Rel: 18 Jul 1969[3]

ACT 4542 BARBARA MASON: Slipping Away / Half A Love
Label: AC1   Rel: unknown

ACT 4543 THE FANTASTIC JOHHNY C: Is There Anything Better Than Making Love / New Love
Label: AC1   Rel: unknown

ACT 4544 JACKIE LEE AND DELORES HALL: Whether It's Right Or Wrong / Baby I'm Satisfied (NOT RELEASED)

ACT 4544 THE HIDEAWAYS: Hideout / Jolly Joe
Label: see below   Rel: 24 Oct 1969[3]
Catalogue number originally assigned to *Whether It's Right Or Wrong / Baby I'm Satisfied* by Jackie Lee and Delores Hall, which was instead issued on B&C as CB 105 with "ACT 4544" crossed out in the run–off. Confirmed on second label design, but if release date is correct, then this must exist on the first label design.

ACT 4545 NORMAN JOHNSON AND THE SHOWMEN: Take It Baby / In Paradise
Label: AC1   Rel: 19 Sep 1969[3]
The US Swan label issue was credited to "The Showmen" alone.

ACT 4546 THE WASH HOPSON SINGERS: He's Got A Blessing / Rocking In A Weary Land
Label: AC1   Rel: 18 Jul 1969[3]

ACT 4547 EDDIE HOLMAN: I Love You / I Surrender
Label: AC1   Rel: 22 Aug 1969[3]

ACT 4548 BOBBY BLAND: Share Your Love With Me / Honey Child
Label: pres. AC1   Rel: 22 Aug 1969[3]

ACT 4549 CLIFFORD CURRY: She Shot A Hole In My Soul / We're Gonna Hate Ourselves In The Morning
Label: AC1   Rel: 3 Oct 1969[3]

ACT 4550 CLIFTON CHENIER: Black Girl / Frog Legs
Label: Rel: 31 Oct 1969[3]

ACT 4551 GENE CHANDLER: I Can't Save It / I Can Take Care Of Myself
Label: pres. AC1   Rel: 24 Oct 1969[3]

ACT 4552 THE PERFORMERS: I Can't Stop You / L.A. Stomp
Label: AC1   Rel: 31 Oct 1969[3]

The last single on the orange label design? Also exists on the black/green design. Orange label copies credit "Mirwood Recording" whilst black/green label copies credit "Crestview/Mirwood Recording".

ACT 4553   **BOBBY BLAND: Chains Of Love / Ask Me 'Bout Nothing But The Blues**
Label: AC2   **Rel:** 21 Nov 1969[3]

ACT 4554   **NO RELEASE**

ACT 4555   **EDDIE WILSON: Get Out On The Street / Must Be Love**
Label: AC2   **Rel:** 13 Feb 1970[3]

ACT 4556   **THE OLYMPICS: I'll Do A Little Bit More / Same Old Thing**
Label: AC2   **Rel:** 13 Feb 1970[3]

ACT 4557   **JEANETTE WILLIAMS: Hound Dog / I Can Feel A Heartbreak**
Label: AC2   **Rel:** 27 Feb 1970[3]

ACT 4600 sequence 7" singles

The end of the 4500 sequence almost certainly represents the point at which John Abbey ceased his involvement with B&C/Action and moved on to Polydor via the Contempo label. After a year and a half the label was revived along the same lines but now with a few reggae releases dotted amongst the usual soul fare.

ACT 4601   **NORMAN JOHNSON AND THE SHOWMEN: You're Everything / Our Love Will Grow**
Label: AC2   **Rel:** 1 Oct 1971[3]
Reissue of ACT 4529

ACT 4602   **BILLY SHA–RAE: Do It / Crying Clown**
Label: AC2   **Rel:** 5 Nov 1971[3]
Copies exist with both four prong die–cut and solid centres.

ACT 4603   **BOBBETTES: That's A Bad Thing To Know / All In Your Mind**
Label: AC2   **Rel:** 14 Jan[8]/28 Jan 1972[3]

ACT 4604   **BOBBY PATTERSON: I'm In Love With You / Married Lady**
Label: AC2   **Rel:** 3 Mar[3]/7 Apr 1972[3]

ACT 4605   **HOAGY LANDS: Why Didn't You Let Me Know / Do You Know What Life Is All About**
Label: AC2   **Rel:** 19 May 1972[3]

ACT 4606   **KIM FOWLEY: Born To Make You Cry / Thunder Road**
Label: AC2   **Rel:** 3 May[3]/21 Jul[8]/4 Aug 1972[3]
Stock copies exist with solid centres.

ACT 4607   **JOE S. MAXEY: Sign Of The Crab / May The Best Man Win**
Label: AC2   **Rel:** May 1973[5]

ACT 4608   **THE SINGING PRINCIPAL: Thank You Baby / Women's Lib**
Label: AC2   **Rel:** 4 May 1973[8]

The B&C Discography: 1968 to 1975

ACT 4609   **EDDIE BO: Check Your Bucket Part One / Check Your Bucket Part Two**
Label: AC3   **Rel:** 1 Jun 1973[8]
Three variations known: solid–centred promotional copies exist with "DEMO RECORD NOT FOR SALE" text and tracks the same as on the normal stock release; four prong die–cut centred promotional copies exist with just a large block "A" and tracks the same as on the normal stock release; normal die–cut centred stock copies viewed seem to have much rougher textured labels than the promotional variations.

ACT 4610   **GAYTONES: Soul Makossa Part 1 / Soul Makossa Part 2**
Label: AC3   **Rel:** 6 Jul 1973[3]
Promotional copies have a large block "A", though otherwise the same as the normal stock release.

ACT 4611   **JAMAICA BAND: Sticky Fingers / Sticky Fingers. Part 2**
Label: AC3   **Rel:** 17 Aug 1973[3]
Promotional copies exist with a large block "A", though tracks are the same as on the normal stock release, and have a noticeably rougher texture label than other releases around this date. That this is an Orlake pressing, even though B&C was generally using EMI to press records at this point, is confirmed by the "ACT+4611+A" / "ACT+4611+B" matrix numbers in the run–off.

ACT 4612   **BUSTER PEARSON BAND: Big Funk / Pretty Woman**
Label: AC3   **Rel:** 24 Aug 1973[3]
Promotional copies exist with a large block "A", though with same tracks as on normal stock release.

ACT 4613   **WILBERT HARRISON: Get It While You Can / Amen**
Label: AC4   **Rel:** 12 Oct 1973[3]

ACT 4614   **5 MILES OUT: Super Sweet Girl Of Mine / Set Your Mind Free**
Label: AC4   **Rel:** 26 Oct 1973[3]
One–sided white label test pressing exists.

ACT 4615   **STANLEY: I'll Go Down And Getcha Pt 1 / I'll Go Down And Getcha Pt 2**
Label: AC4   **Rel:** 2 Nov 1973[3]
Promotional copies exist with track listing as above.

ACT 4616   **BACKYARD HEAVIES: Just Keep On Truckin' / Never Can Say Goodbye**
Label: AC4   **Rel:** 9 Nov[3]/30 Nov 1973[3]
Promotional copies exist with *My Sweet Baby* on both sides though some play normal b–side.

ACT 4617   **MILL EDWARDS: I Found Myself / Don't Forget About Me**
Label: AC4   **Rel:** 9 Nov 1973[3]

ACT 4618   **THE ESQUIRES: My Sweet Baby / Henry Ralph**
Label: AC4   **Rel:** 16 Nov 1973[3]

ACT 4619   **AARON McNEIL: Soul Of A Black Man / Reap What You Sow**
Label: AC4   **Rel:** 16 Nov 1973[3]

ACT 4620   **CHUCK ARMSTRONG: Black Foxy Woman / God Bless The Children**
Label: AC4   **Rel:** 11 Jan 1974[3]   **Del:** 1978[5]
Promotional copies exist with *Black Foxy Woman* on both labels, though some play normal b–side.

ACT 4621 TOM GREEN: Rock Springs Railroad Station / Endless Confusion
Label: AC4 Rel: 11 Jan 1974[3] Del: 1976[5]

ACT 4622 BOBBIE HOUSTON: I Want To Make It With You / I Want To Make It With You (Instrumental)
Label: AC4 Rel: 11 Jan 1974[3]

ACT 4623 THE CHOSEN FEW: Funky Butter / Wondering
Label: AC4 Rel: 11 Jan 1974[3] Del: 1976[5]

ACT 4624 WEE WILLIE AND THE WINNERS: Get Some / A Plan For The Man
Label: AC4 Rel: 19 Apr 1974[3]
Orlake pressings known to exist.

ACT 100 sequence 7" singles

After yet another hiatus, this time of just over a year, the Action label was brought back into service, this time as an output for what B&C and Trojan referred to as 'ethnic reggae'. The label was not resurrected following B&C and Trojan's liquidation.

ACT 101 BIG YOUTH: Knotty No Jester / Knotty No Jester (Instrumental)
Label: AC4 Rel: 23 May 1975[3] Del: 1978[5]
Rumours of copies appearing on Trojan's Attack label by mistake are not confirmed.

ACT 102 CORNELL CAMPBELL: Natty Dread In A Greenwich Farm / Natty Version
Label: AC4 Rel: 6 Jun 1975[3] Del: 1977[5]

ACT 103 LINVAL THOMPSON: Natty Dread Girl / Natty Dread Girl (Version)
Label: AC4 Rel: not notified to *The New Singles*

Promotional 7" EP

This was used for promotional singles over several B&C–related labels. Most so far identified were of artists on B&C, Charisma or Pegasus/Peg. Only one record has been discovered with Action label material, and that only on one side with the other dedicated to People label material. All tracks are excerpts.

BCP 16 VARIOUS ARTISTS: untitled
1. Forever (Don Gardner And Baby Washington)
2. Lonely Days, Lonely Nights (Don Downing)
1. Check Your Bucket (Eddie Bo)
2. Get It While You Can (Wilbert Harrison)
Label: see below

The a–side had the People label design, whilst the b–side was the Action label design (AC3).

Stable

SLP sequence LP

SLP 7001   THE DEVIANTS: Disposable (MONO)

1. Somewhere To Go
2. Sparrows And Wires
3. Jamie's Song
4. You've Got To Hold On
5. Fire In The City
6. Let's Loot The Supermarket

1. Pappa–Oo–Mao–Mao
2. Slum Lord
3. Blind Joe McTurk's Last Session
4. Normality Jim
5. Guaranteed To Bleed
6. Sidney B. Goode
7. Last Man

Rel: May 1969[1]
RRP: 40/11[1]

Unidentified music paper advert cutting has RRP of 39/11 – RRP as advised above probably incorrect.

SLE sequence LPs

All records listed as stereo in *The New Records* except for SLE 8001. At least two LPs were originally assigned to the B&C label. SLE 8004 was originally assigned to CAS 1004 and SLE 8005 was originally assigned to CAS.1008.

SLE 8001   SAM GOPAL: Escalator (MONO)

1. Cold Embrace
2. The Dark Lord
3. The Sky Is Burning
4. You're Alone Now
5. Grass
6. It's Only Love

1. Escalator
2. Angry Faces
3. Midsummer Night's Dream
4. Season Of The Witch
5. Yesterlove

Rel: Mar 1969[1]
RRP: 37/5[1]

SLE 8002   N.S.U.: Turn Me On, Or Turn Me Down

1. Turn Me On, Or Turn Me Down
2. His Town
3. You Can't Take It From The Heart
4. Love Talk
5. All Aboard

1. The Game
2. Stoned
3. Pettsie's Blues
4. On The Road Again

Rel: Jun/Jul '69[1]
RRP: 37/5[1]

SLE 8003   JAKLIN: Jaklin

1. Rosie
2. Song To Katherine
3. Look For Me Baby
4. Early In The Morning
5. Just Been Left Again

1. The Same For You
2. I Can't Go On
3. Going Home
4. I'm Leaving
5. Catfish Blues

Rel: Oct 1969[1]
RRP: 37/5[1]

SLE 8004   THE VICTIMS OF CHANCE: Victims Of Chance

1. Victims Of Chance, Part 1
2. Victims Of Chance, Part 2
3. Adventures In Tyme
4. Break Away
5. Over And Out (Coda, Side One)

1. Tuesday's Victim
2. L.A. To Frisco – Four Eleven Flat
3. Funky Sunshine
4. Devil's Prayer

Rel: Feb/Mar '70[1]
RRP: 37/5[1]

Licenced from the US Crestview Records label, from which B&C also licensed Bob and Earl.

SLE 8005   THE GROUP IMAGE: A Mouth In The Clouds

1. Aunt Ida
2. A Way To Love You All The Time
3. Voices Calling Me
4. Moonlit Dip
5. New Romancing

1. Hiya
2. Banana Split
3. My Man
4. Grew Up All Wrong
5. The Treat

Rel: Jul 1970[1]
RRP: 39/11[1]

STA sequence 7" single

A single in this sequence by Sam Gopal is rumoured to exist, but no copy has yet come to light so perhaps we can assume that it was not issued. Still, with B&C you never know.

STA 5601   THE DEVIANTS: You've Got To Hold On / Let's Loot The Supermarket

Rel: 22 Nov 1968[3]
Demo copies with "SAMPLE COPY NOT FOR RESALE" text credit side 1 as "You Got to Hold On".

Promotional 7" EP

This record was assigned the same catalogue number as the LP that it was pressed to promote. The matrix numbers started a short–lived B&C trend for assigning promotional records with catalogue numbers derived from the artist name, e.g "JH1" and "JH2" for the promotional single for the Jackson Heights Charisma label LP. Promotional singles for the Genesis, Hannibal and Brian Davison LPs received similar treatment.

SLE 8001 SAM GOPAL

1. Escalator
2. Angry Faces

1. Cold Embrace
2. The Sky Is Burning

Includes "DJ COPY NOT FOR RESALE" and "D.J. SAMPLER From SAM GOPAL L.P. 'ESCALATOR'" on labels. Matrix numbers (included on label) are "SG1–A" and "SG1–B". Both sides are published by B&C Music.

B&C and Charisma

B&C and Charisma shared B&C's two main catalogue sequences, CAS and CB, and both labels used the promotional BCP sequence. As already stated, Charisma releases are shown only until the last B&C label release on each relevant sequence. Full information on Charisma's subsequent B&C–era releases can be found in *The Famous Charisma Discography*, which is also available, with updates, as an eBook.

CAS sequence LPs

The last B&C record on this sequence was CAS 1045 and, despite 1972 listings in trade publications, B&C supposedly ceased using the CAS sequence in September 1971. The last three CAS numbers assigned to B&C, CAS 1046–1048, were not used, though the albums originally assigned the first two numbers appeared on the Pegasus label with the CAS matrix numbers crossed out in the run–off. This did not represent the first instance of B&C–planned releases being transferred to another label. At least two early releases, CAS 1004 and 1008, were transferred to Stable. All records in this sequence still on catalogue as at decimalisation were listed with RRP of £2.14[4] as at February 1971.

CAS 1001   MERRILL MOORE: Tree Top Tall
1. House of Blue Lights – 69
2. Wabash Blues
3. Kansas City
4. Born to Lose
5. Texas In My Soul
6. Bring Me Sunshine

1. Sweet Mama Tree Top Tall
2. Release Me
3. Let the Good Times Roll
4. She Won't Let Me Forget Her
5. Wabash Cannonball
6. Little Green Apples

Label: BC1
Rel: May 1969[1]
RRP: 37/5[1]

CAS 1002   DION AND THE BELMONTS: Together Again
1. Moving Man
2. Berimbau
3. Come To My Side
4. All I Wanna Do
5. But Not for Me
6. New York Town

1. Loserville
2. For Bobbie
3. Jump Back Baby
4. Baby You've Been On My Mind
5. My Girl the Month Of May

Label: BC2
Rel: Oct 1969[1]
RRP: 37/5[1]
Del: Mar 1974[4]

Reissue of HMV label issue, CLP 3618.

CAS 1003   PACIFIC GAS AND ELECTRIC: Get It On
1. Wade In The Water
2. Cry, Cry, Cry
3. Motor City's Burning

1. The Hunter
2. Long Handled Shovel
3. Jelly Jelly
4. Stormy Times
5. Live Love

Label: BC2
Rel: Oct 1969[1]
RRP: 37/5[1]
Del: Mar 1974[4]

CAS 1004   VICTIMS OF CHANCE: Victims Of Chance (NOT RELEASED)
Instead issued on Stable as SLE 8004 with "CAS 1004" crossed out in the run–off.

CAS 1005   RARE BIRD: Rare Bird (Charisma)
1. Iceberg
2. Times
3. You Went Away
4. Melanie

1. Beautiful Scarlet
2. Sympathy
3. Natures Fruit
4. Bird On A Wing
5. God Of War

Label: CH1
Rel: Dec 1969[1]
RRP: 37/6[1]
Del: Mar 1975[4]

The B&C Discography: 1968 to 1975

There is also documentation of a November 1969 release date[6] though this looks to be incorrect. The above–listed December date is most likely, especially as Gail Colson, Charisma's then label manager gives: a release date of December 10th (email dated 2nd July 2009).

CAS 1006   NO RELEASE

CAS 1007   VAN DER GRAAF GENERATOR: The Least We Can Do Is Wave to Each Other (Charisma)

1. Darkness (11/11)
2. Refugees
3. White Hammer

1. Whatever Would Robert Have Said
2. Out Of My Book
3. After the Flood

Label: CH1
Rel: Jan[6]/Feb '70[1]
RRP: 37/5[1]

Two different mixes exist on the original, rough–textured label design. A double–sided poster was included with first mix and some second mix copies. Original mix copies have "CAS+1007+A2" and "CAS+1007+B2" matrix numbers, denoting these to be Orlake pressings. The original mix is fairly odd with vocals, drums, and bass to the fore but little evidence of the organ or saxophone. The ending to *After the Flood* is significantly different, with a complete fade out before the final organ scrunge. Remixed scroll label copies have the matrix numbers "CAS+1007+A+G" and "CAS+1007+B+G". Second mix copies on smooth–textured pink scroll label have "A–3U" and "B–3U" matrix suffixes, denoting these to be EMI pressings. By this time the label includes the B&C credit. B&C–era copies did not include sleeve spine credits. This LP also appears in the Oct 1970 edition of *The New Records* with a price of 39/11. This might indicate the date that the remixed version appeared.

CAS 1008   THE GROUP IMAGE: A Mouth In The Clouds (NOT RELEASED)
Instead issued on Stable as SLE 8005 with "CAS 1008" crossed out in the run–off.

CAS 1008   JOSEPH EGER: Classical Heads (Charisma)

1. Lelio (Berlioz/Eger):
    ii Chorus Of The Shades
    iv Fantasia On Shakespeare's
        Tempest
2. Symphonie Fantastique (Excerpts)
    (Berlioz/Eger):
    1st Movement
    4th Movement
    5th Century Plain Song

1. Symphonie Fantastique:
    5th Movement
2. The Unanswered Question (Ives)
3. Sonata Pia E. Forte (Gabriele)
4. Troika (From Leuitenant Kije)
5. Infernal Dance Of Kastchei
    (Stravinsky)

Label: CH1
Rel: Mar[6]/Apr '70[1]
RRP: 39/11[1]

Labels credit "The Sinfonia of London with the Ambrosian Singers, words spoken by John Neville". On catalogue long enough to be issued on the large Mad Hatter label (though still as an Orlake, rather than EMI, pressing).

CAS 1009   GORDON TURNER: Meditation (Charisma)

1. A System Of Meditation By
    Threefold Attunement
    And Text Spoken By
    Gordon Turner

1. A System Of Meditation By
    Threefold Attunement
    And Text Spoken By
    Gordon Turner

Label: CH1
Rel: Mar[6]/Apr '70[1]
RRP: 39/11[1]

Subtitled, "A System of Meditation By Three–fold Attunement", this was issued in two different sleeve designs, both of which included a 16 page booklet. The front sleeve of the first issue included a colourful picture of a dragonfly – the front only was laminated; the second (unlaminated) sleeve design was of a window in a bare room. The text and layout on the rear of the sleeve differed between the two designs. The first press in the laminated sleeve was an Orlake pressing, whilst all copies of the second press in the non–laminated sleeve viewed have been Philips pressings. This is one of only two confirmed Philips LP pressings for B&C/Charisma. Neither issue includes B&C label credits.

The B&C Discography: 1968 to 1975

CAS 1010 **ATOMIC ROOSTER: Atomic Rooster**

1. Friday The 13th	1. Banstead	**Label:** BC2
2. And So To Bed	2. S.L.Y.	**Rel:** Mar 1970[1]
3. Broken Wings	3. Winter	**RRP:** 37/5[1]
4. Before Tomorrow	4. Decline And Fall	

Also appears in the October 1970 edition of *The New Records* with a price of 39/11 – and it is possible that this date represents a repromotion of the album following remixing and overdubbing of vocals and guitar. There are generally known to be two versions of the album, one referred to as the "flute mix" and the other as the "guitar mix". The reason for the two mixes is that new member, John Cann, added vocals and guitar to *Friday the 13th* and guitar to *S.L.Y.* and *Before Tomorrow* prior to the album's US release on Elektra. These new versions subsequently replaced the original tracks on the UK issue. However, just to confuse issues, there are actually two different flute mixes to contend with as well, with tracks switched between sides, depending on mix version. There is also a very interesting mispress that mixes both 'flute mix' variations.

There's quite a lot to unravel about the different versions, but the above track listing represents that as listed on all labels and sleeves – these seem to have remained consistent throughout all variations. This means that sleeve and labels showed an incorrect track listing on the very first press. Exact order of tracks on original copies is not yet confirmed – first 'flute mix' copies (Orlake pressings with "CAS+1010+A"/"CAS+1010+B" matrix numbers in the run-offs) had *Broken Wings* (definitely) and *Before Tomorrow* (probably) on side 2 and *Winter* and *Decline And Fall* (both definitely) on side 1.

The LP seems to have been hurriedly remixed with tracks moved so as to follow the track listing as listed on sleeve and labels (as shown above). This second 'flute mix' is also an Orlake pressing and has "CAS+1010+A2"/ "CAS+1010+B2" matrix numbers in the run-offs – and it is probably worth mentioning that the run-off space is wider on this version than on the original press, the grooves being more compacted. The 'guitar mix' version included the remixed and overdubbed versions of *Friday the 13th*, *S.L.Y.* and *Before Tomorrow*. All known 'guitar mix' copies are EMI pressings with "CAS 1010 A–1U"/"CAS 1010 B–1U" matrix numbers in the run-off.

One super-rare variation has surfaced recently, which is a hybrid of the two 'flute mix' versions with "CAS+1010+A" matrix on side 1 and "CAS+1010+B2" matrix on side 2. This means that the record has *Winter* and *Decline And Fall* on both sides of the record, with different mixes on each side.

CAS 1011 **RARE BIRD: As Your Mind Flies By (Charisma)**

1. What You Want to Know	1. Flight:	**Label:** CH2
2. Down on the Floor	Part 1: As Your Mind Flies By	**Rel:** Sep[6]/Oct '70[1]
3. Hammerhead	Part 2: Vacuum	**RRP:** 39/11[1]
4. I'm Thinking	Part 3: New Yorker	
	Part 4: Central Park	

Textured sleeve.

CAS 1012 **AUDIENCE: Friend's Friend's Friend (Charisma)**

1. Nothing You Do	1. Right On Their Side	**Label:** CH1
2. Belladonna Moonshine	2. Ebony Variations	**Rel:** May[6]/Oct'70[1]
3. It Brings a Tear	3. Priestess	**RRP:** 39/11[1]
4. Raid	4. Friend's, Friend's, Friend	

The release date in *The New Records* may represent a renotification of release.

CAS 1013 **NO RELEASE**

The B&C Discography: 1968 to 1975

CAS 1014   THE NICE: Five Bridges (Charisma)

1. The Five Bridges Suite:
    Fantasia. 1st Bridge
    2nd Bridge
    Chorale. 3rd Bridge
    High Level Fugue. 4th Bridge
    Finale. 5th Bridge

1. Intermezzo, Karelia Suite
2. Pathetique Symphony No. 6
    3rd Movement
3. Country Pie/Brandenburg Concerto
    No. 6
4. One Of Those People

Label: CH1
Rel: May 1970[1]
RRP: £2.14[4]

Cassette: ZCCAS 1014
8–track: Y8CAS 1014

Rel: Apr 1972[2]
Rel: Apr 1972[2]

RRP: £2.50[2]
RRP: £2.60[2]

One of only two B&C/Charisma LPs to be confirmed with Philips pressings.

CAS 1015   KEITH CHRISTMAS: Fable Of The Wings

1. Waiting For The Wind To Rise
2. The Fawn
3. Lorri

1. Kent Lullaby
2. Hamlin
3. Fable Of The Wings
4. Bednotch

Label: BC3
Rel: Nov 1970[1]
RRP: 39/11[1]

Embossed sleeve with photos affixed to front and rear. For those who insist on trivia, the photos were taken in part of Magic Muscle's squat in the Cotham area of Bristol.

CAS 1016   HAROLD McNAIR: The Fence

1. The Fence
2. True Love Adventure
3. Early In The Morning

1. Scarborough Fair
2. Here, There And Everywhere

Label: BC3
Rel: Nov 1970[1]
RRP: 39/11[1]
Del: Mar 1974[4]

Most copies have a torn sleeve where a pink pouch was attached complete with party balloon inside.

CAS 1017   TREVOR BILLMUSS: Family Apology (Charisma)

1. Ground Song
2. Reflections On Lady Macbeth
3. The Viennese Carousel
4. Last September
5. Sunday Afternoon In Belgrave
    Square
6. Hungarian Peasant Girl
7. Epithaph For Matthew

1. Whoops Amour
2. The Flaming Bossa Nova
3. Casual Friends
4. Pousette
5. Fishing Song
6. Wise Eyes

Label: CH2
Rel: Sep[6]/Oct '70[1]
RRP: 39/11[1]
Del: Mar 1975[4]

Textured sleeve. Neither this (nor the singles, one on Charisma and the other on B&C) sold despite a large recording budget. If this had appeared on Immediate, Harvest or Vertigo, it would now be hailed as a masterpiece. Well, a masterpiece it remains, and with no reissue to date, an obscure and incredibly rare masterpiece, the price of which is starting to reflect its quality and scarcity.

CAS 1018   JACKSON HEIGHTS: King Progress (Charisma)

1. Mr. Screw
2. Since I Last Saw You
3. Sunshine Freak
4. King Progress

1. Doubting Thomas
2. Insomnia
3. Cry Of Eugene

Label: CH2
Rel: Oct[6]/Nov '70[1]
RRP: 39/11[1]
Del: Mar 1975[4]

CAS 1019   SHELAGH McDONALD: Album

1. Mirage
2. Look Over The Hill And Far Away
3. Crusoe
4. Waiting For The Wind to Rise
5. Ophelia's Song (Version 1)

1. Richmond
2. Let No Man Steal Your Thyme
3. Peacock Lady
4. Silk And Leather
5. You Know You Can't Lose

Label: BC3
Rel: Nov 1970[1]
RRP: 39/11[1]
Del: Mar 1974[4]

CAS 1020   GENESIS: Trespass (Charisma)

1. Looking For Someone	1. Stagnation	**Label:** CH2
2. White Mountain	2. Dusk	**Rel:** Oct[6]/Nov '70[1]
3. Visions Of Angels	3. The Knife	**RRP:** 39/11[1]

Cassette: ZCCAS 1020   **Rel:** not advised   **RRP:** unknown
8–track: Y8CAS 1020   **Rel:** not advised   **RRP:** unknown

Original pink scroll and early large Mad Hatter copies issued in textured sleeve with insert on flimsy, lightly–textured, light green paper. The insert was later printed on thicker, white paper. Tape versions not notified to the trade but an 8–track cartridge issue is confirmed, which would suggest that a cassette version was also issued – all Charisma product at this point was issued in both tape formats when issued on tape at all. Advertising inner sleeves from July/August 1972 do not list *Trespass* as issued on tape, so quite when the tape versions were released is unknown. Perhaps they were issued in the wake of the success of *Foxtrot*, which was issued in the September.

CAS 1021   BRIAN DAVISON'S EVERY WHICH WAY: Every Which Way (Charisma)

1. Bed Ain't What It Used To Be	1. All In Time	**Label:** CH2
2. Castle Sand	2. What You Like	**Rel:** Sep[6]/Oct '70[1]
3. Go Placidly	3. The Light	**RRP:** 39/11[1]

The record spine credited the LP to "Brian Davison", whilst the back sleeve and the labels credited "Brian Davison's Every Which Way". There was no credit on the front sleeve. Copies exist with the labels affixed to the wrong sides.

CAS 1022   HANNIBAL: Hannibal

1. Look Upon Me	1. 1066	**Label:** BC3
2. Winds Of Change	2. Wet Legs	**Rel:** Nov 1970[1]
3. Bend For A Friend	3. Winter	**RRP:** 39/11[1]
		Del: Mar 1974[4]

CAS 1023   CAROL GRIMES AND DELIVERY: Fool's Meeting

1. Blind To Your Light	1. We Were Satisfied	**Label:** BC3
2. Miserable Man	2. The Wrong Time	**Rel:** Nov 1970[1]
3. Home Made Ruin	3. Fighting It Out	**RRP:** 39/11[1]
4. Is It Really The Same	4. Fool's Meeting	**Del:** Mar 1974[4]

Appears in the January 1971 edition of *The New Records* with the same RRP (listed under Charisma).

CAS 1024   STEAMHAMMER: Mountains

1. I Wouldn't Have Thought (Gophers Song)	1 Leader Of The Ring	**Label:** BC3
2. Levinia	2. Riding On The L And M	**Rel:** Nov 1970[1]
3. Henry Lane	3. Hold That Train	**RRP:** 39/11[1]
4. Walking Down The Road		**Del:** Mar 1974[4]
5. Mountains		

Sleeve included a sticker with album credits and a picture of the band, otherwise there were no credits anywhere on the outer sleeve, though credits appeared on the inner gatefold.

CAS 1025   LINDISFARNE: Nicely Out Of Tune (Charisma)

1. Lady Eleanor	1. We Can Swing Together	**Label:** CH2
2. Road To Kingdom Come	2. Alan In The River With Flowers	**Rel:** Oct[6]/Nov '70[1]
3. Winter Song	3. Down	**RRP:** 39/11[1]
4. Turn A Deaf Ear	4. The Things I Should Have Said	
5. Clear White Light – Part 2	5. Jackhammer Blues	
	6. Scarecrow Song	

The B&C Discography: 1968 to 1975

Cassette: ZCCAS 1025   **Rel:** Apr 1972[2]   **RRP:** £2.50[2]
8–track: Y8CAS 1025   **Rel:** Apr 1972[2]   **RRP:** £2.60[2]
Textured sleeve.

CAS 1026   ATOMIC ROOSTER: Death Walks Behind You

1. Death Walks Behind You
2. Vug
3. Tomorrow Night
4. Streets

1. Sleeping For Years
2. I Can't Take No More
3. Nobody Else
4. Gershatzer

Label: see below
Rel: Nov 1970[1]
RRP: 39/11[1]

One label was the usual BC3 design, whilst the other label was customised with a graveyard–set band photo. This author, writing for *The Rough Guide To Rock*, described this as, "The album that defined the Rooster image as dark, satanic, leather–clad, moody and magnificent. From the opening freaky piano solo and scrunchy guitar to the final crashing chord, this album is the epitome of heavy rock (as distinct from heavy metal)."

CAS 1027   VAN DER GRAAF GENERATOR: H To He, Who Am the Only One (Charisma)

1. Killer
2. House With No Door
3. The Emperor In His War Room:
    i) The Emperor
    ii) The Room

1. Lost:
    i) The Dance In Sand And Sea
    ii) The Dance In Frost
2. Pioneers Over C

Label: CH2
Rel: Dec 1970[6]/
    Jan 1971[1]
RRP: 39/11[1]

CAS 1028   EVERYONE: Everyone

1. Trouble At Mill
2. Sad
3. Midnight Shift
4. Don't Get Me Wrong

1. Sitting On A Rock
2. Too Much A Loser
3. Radio Lady
4. This Way Up

Label: BC3
Rel: Feb 1971[1]
RRP: £2.15[1]
Del: Mar 1974[4]

The first CAS LP to be listed with a decimal price. Listed under Charisma in *The New Records*.

CAS 1029   STEELEYE SPAN: Please To See The King

1. The Blacksmith
2. Cold, Haily, Windy Night
3. Jigs: Bryan O'Lynn/The Hag With The Money
4. Prince Charlie Stewart
5. Boys Of Bedlam

1. False Knight On The Road
2. The Lark In The Morning
3. Female Drummer
4. The King
5. Lovely In The Water

Label: BC3
Rel: unknown
RRP: prob. £2.15

Cassette: ZCPEG 1029   **Rel:** Jul 1972[2]   **RRP:** £2.25[2]
8–track: Y8PEG 1029   **Rel:** Jul 1972[2]   **RRP:** £2.35[2]

Hessian–feel sleeve. This included an insert with explanatory notes, which, still with B&C credits, was included with a few early 1974 Mooncrest (CREST 8) copies. By the time the tape versions were issued B&C label artists had been transferred to the Pegasus/Peg label. Therefore this and subsequent tape releases were given the PEG prefix in place of CAS, though retaining their original catalogue number.

CAS 1030   THE NICE: Elegy (Charisma)

1. Hang On To A Dream
2. My Back Pages

1. 3rd Movement Pathetique
2. America 2nd Amendment

Label: CH2
Rel: Apr[6]/May '71[1]
RRP: £2.15[1]

Cassette: ZCCAS 1030   **Rel:** not advised?   **RRP:** unknown
8–track: Y8CAS 1030   **Rel:** not advised?   **RRP:** unknown

The B&C Discography: 1968 to 1975

CAS 1031   **GINHOUSE: Ginhouse**

1. Tyne God
2. I Cannot Understand
3. The Journey
4. Portrait Picture
5. Fair Stood the Wind

1. And I Love Her
2. Life
3. Morning After
4. House
5. Sun In A Bottle

Label: BC3
Rel: Apr 1971[1]
RRP: £2.15[1]
Del: Mar 1974[4]

Listed under Charisma in *The New Records*.

CAS 1032   **AUDIENCE: The House On The Hill (Charisma)**

1. Jackdaw
2. Youre Not Smilin'
3. I Had A Dream
4. Raviole

1. Nancy
2. Eye To Eye
3. I Put A Spell On You
4. The House On The Hill

Label: CH2
Rel: Apr[6]/May '71[1]
RRP: £2.15[1]

Cassette: ZCCAS 1032   **Rel:** unknown   **RRP:** unknown
8–track: Y8CAS 1032   **Rel:** unknown   **RRP:** unknown

Inner sleeve. Tape versions do not seem to have been advised to *The New Cassettes and Cartridges*.

CAS 1033   **MARC ELLINGTON: Rains/Reins Of Changes**

1. Oh No It Can't Be So
2. On Your Own
3. Saving Grace
4. Song For A Friend
5. Yarrow
6. I'm Leaving (America)

1. Rains/Reins Of Changes
2. The Life You Love
3. Days Used To Be Much Warmer
4. Alligator Man
5. All The Times
6. Blue Suede Shoes

Label: BC3
Rel: Jun 1971[1]
RRP: £2.15[1]
Del: Mar 1974[4]

Top–opening, textured sleeve plus insert.

CAS 1034   **ANDY ROBERTS: Home Grown**

1. Home Grown
2. Just For The Record
3. Applecross
4. John The Revelator
5. Moths and Lizards In Detroit

1. Creepy John
2. Gig Song
3. Queen Of The Moonlight World
4. Lonely In The Crowd
5. The One–Armed Boatman And The Giant Squid

Label: BC3
Rel: Jun 1971[1]
RRP: £2.15[1]
Del: Mar 1974[4]

Gatefold insert.

CAS 1035   **TIM HART AND MADDY PRIOR: Summer Solstice**

1. False Knight On The Road
2. Bring Us In Good Ale
3. Of All The Birds
4. I Live Not Where I Love
5. The Ploughboy And The Cockney
6. Westron Wynde

1. Sorry The Day I Was Married
2. Dancing At Whitsun
3. Fly Up My Cock
4. Cannily Cannily
5. Adam Catched Eve
6. Three Drunken Maidens
7. Serving–Girls Holiday

Label: BC3
Rel: Jun 1971[1]
RRP: £2.15[1]

Cassette: ZCPEG 1035   **Rel:** Jul 1972[2]   **RRP:** £2.25[2]
8–track: Y8PEG 1035   **Rel:** Jul 1972[2] (del: 1977[5])   **RRP:** £2.35[2]

CAS 1036   **BIRTH CONTROL: Birth Control (Charisma)**

1. Stop Little Lady
2. Just Before The Sun Will Rise
3. The Work Is Done

1. Flesh And Blood
2. Pandemonium
3. Let Us Do It Now

Label: CH2
Rel: May[6]/Jun '71[1]
RRP: £2.15[1]

The B&C Discography: 1968 to 1975

CAS 1037   PETER HAMMILL: Fool's Mate (Charisma)

1. Imperial Zeppelin
2. Candle
3. Happy
4. Solitude
5. Vision
6. Re–Awakening

1. Sunshine
2. Child
3. Summer Song (In The Autumn)
4. Viking
5. The Birds
6. I Once Wrote Some Poems

Label: CH2
Rel: Jun[6]/Jul '71[1]
RRP: £2.15[1]

Textured sleeve.

CAS 1038   WISHFUL THINKING: Hiroshima

1. Hiroshima
2. She Belongs To The Night
3. Mary Goodbye
4. Ever Since I Can Remember
5. We're Going To Change All This

1. Now
2. United States Of Europe 79
3. I Wrote A Song
4. 1984
5. Goodbye Lover

Label: BC3
Rel: 1971
RRP: £2.14[4]
Del: Mar 1974[4]

CAS 1039   ATACAMA: Atacama (Charisma)

1. Fiesta A Himara (Bolivia)
2. El Arbol (Chile)
3. A Las Orillas Del Titicaca (Peru)
4. Atara (Argentina)
5. Ojos Azules (Chile)
6. Canto Del Cuculi (Chile)

1. Yaravi Y Huayno De La Quebrada De Humahuaca (Agentina)
2. Dos Palomitas – Yaravi, Huayno, Cueca (Argentina)
3. El Canelazo (Ecuador)
4. Toccoro (Peru)
5. Por Una Pequena Chispa (Bolivia)
6. Virgenes Del Sol (Peru)

Label: CH2
Rel: Jun[6]/Jul '71[1]
RRP: £2.15[1]
Del: Mar 1975[4]

Originally released in the UK in 1970 on the Music Network Label (MNWL-10P) with a different sleeve.

CAS 1040   LEIGH STEPHENS: Leigh Stephens And A Cast Of Thousands (Charisma)

1. World Famous Soul Transplant
2. Medicine Man
3. Simple Song
4. Handful Of Friends

1. Oh Lord
2. Jumpin' Jack Flash
3. Sweet Love Of Mind
4. Chunk Of Funk

Label: CH2
Rel: Aug[6]/Sep '71[1]
RRP: £2.15[1]

CAS 1041   KEITH CHRISTMAS: Pygmy

1. Travelling Down
2. Timeless And Strange
3. Evensong
4. Spanky
5. Poem

1. The Waiting Grounds
2. Song For A Survivor
3. Forest And The Shore

Label: BC3
Rel: Sep 1971[1]
RRP: £2.15[1]
Del: Mar 1974[4]

Exists as two one–sided, white label test pressings. Listed under Charisma in *The New Records*.

CAS 1042   SPIROGYRA: St. Radigunds

1. The Future Won't Be Long
2. Island
3. Magical Mary
4. Captains Log
5. At Home In The World

1. Cogwheels, Crutches And Cyanide
2. Time Will Tell
3. We Were A Happy Crew
4. Love Is A Funny Thing
5. The Duke Of Beaufoot

Label: BC3
Rel: Sep 1971[1]
RRP: £2.15[1]
Del: Mar 1974[4]

Inner sleeve. Exists as two one–sided, white label test pressings. Listed under Charisma in *The New Records*.

CAS 1043 SHELAGH McDONALD: Stargazer

1. Rod's Song
2. Liz's Song
3. Lonely King
4. City's Cry
5. Dowie Dens Of Yarrow

1. Baby Go Slow
2. Canadian Man
3. Good Times
4. Odyssey
5. Stargazer

Label: BC3
Rel: Sep 1971 [1]
RRP: £2.15 [1]
Del: Mar 1974 [4]

Inner sleeve. Two one–sided, white label test pressings exist. Listed under Charisma in *The New Records*.

CAS 1044 PAUL KENT: Paul Kent

1. All Across The Night
2. Do You
3. Don't Seduce Your Best Friend's Wife
4. Cool Surprise
5. Soulful Soldier

1. Upstairs Coming Down
2. Rainy Day
3. Song Of Songs
4. Crying In The Aisles
5. Helpless Harry

Label: BC3
Rel: Sep 1971 [1]
RRP: £2.15 [1]
Del: Mar 1974 [4]

Exists as two one–sided, white label test pressings. Listed under Charisma in *The New Records*.

CAS 1045 HAROLD McNAIR: Harold McNair

1. Mento
2. Indecision
3. Lord Of The Reedy River

1. The Hipster
2. Mini Blues
3. Spacecraft
4. The Cottage

Label: BC3
Rel: Feb/Apr '72 [1]
RRP: see below
Del: Mar 1976 [4]

Cassette: ZCPEG 1045   **Rel:** May 1972 [2]   **RRP:** £2.25 [2]
8–track: Y8PEG 1045   **Rel:** May 1972 [2]   **RRP:** £2.35 [2]

Notified to *The New Records* well after B&C had supposedly moved all bar budget releases to Pegasus. *The New Records* RRP is £2.30, whilst *Music Master*'s is £2.14 [4], which is more in line with late 1971 releases. Listed first under Charisma in *The New Records*, then under B&C in April.

CAS 1046 DAVE SWARBRICK AND MARTIN CARTHY: Selections (NOT RELEASED)

Issued instead on B&C's Pegasus label as PEG 6.

CAS 1047 SHIRLEY COLLINS AND THE ALBION COUNTRY BAND: No Roses (NOT RELEASED)

Issued instead on B&C's Pegasus label as PEG 7.

CAS 1048 NO RELEASE

BCB sequence LP

Only one LP issued in the budget–priced series, though B&C/Pegasus material was later issued on the budget Charisma Perspective series. *The Famous Charisma Discography* includes information on Charisma Perspective releases. Probably released earlier than indicated below, based on label design, but *Budget Price Records* indicated below is the first publication in which release is documented. The June edition listed RRP of 15/6!

BCB 101 BOB AND EARL: Bob And Earl

1. Your Time Is My Time (Both)
2. Big Brother (Bob)
3. The Duck (Earl)
4. Baby It's Over (Both)
5. Land Of 1000 Dances (Earl)

1. Puppet On A String (Both)
2. Would You Believe (Earl)
3. My Little Girl (Bob)
4. I'll Keep Running Back (Both)
5. Ooh Honey Baby (Earl)

Label: BC1
Rel: quarter prior to Mar 1970 [9]
RRP: 14/6 [9]

BCM sequence LPs

The BCM mid-priced catalogue sequence outlasted B&C's CAS sequence, with records released long after CAS sequence artists had been transferred to Pegasus. All records listed as stereo in *The New Records* except for BCM 100.

BCM 100   FREDDIE PRIDE: At The Piano (MONO)

1, Take The A Train
2. You Go To My Head
3. A Foggy Day
4. Tenderly
5. Tea For Two
6. Blue Moon
7. Caravan

1. I Can't Give You Anything But Love Baby
2. S'Wonderful
3. There Will Never Be Another You
4. Stars Fell On Alabama
5. If I Had You
6. Please Don't Talk About Me When I'm Gone
7. Laura

Label: BC2
Rel: Feb 1970[1]
RRP: 19/11[1]

BCM 101   WILD ANGELS: Live At The Revolution

1. Johnny B. Goode
2. Great Balls of Fire
3. Summertime Blues
4. Jailhouse Rock
5. Say Mama
6. Mean Woman Blues

1. Jeanie Jeanie Jeanie
2. Matchbox
3. Long Tall Sally
4. Cut Across Shorty
5. Rock Around the Clock
6. Whole Lotta Shakin' Goin' On

Label: BC2
Rel: Mar/May '70[1]
RRP: 19/11[1]

Cassette: ZCBCB 101   **Rel:** Dec 1972[2]   **RRP:** £1.49[2]
8–track: Y8BCB 101   **Rel:** Dec 1972[2]   **RRP:** £1.49[2]

This live album is introduced by Rocking Rosco, who gets a credit under the track listing on the sleeve. The sleeve credits the catalogue number as "B.C.M. 101". Labels are rough textured.

BCM 102   WILD ANGELS: Red Hot 'N' Rockin'

1. Little Queenie
2. Stuck On You
3. Somethin' Else
4. Forty Days
5. Odessa
6. Let the Four Winds Blow

1. High School Confidential
2. All Shook Up
3. You Ain't Got Me
4. I Need Your Love Tonight
5. Rave On
6. Bullmoose

Label: BC3
Rel: Nov 1970[1]
RRP: 19/11[1]

Cassette: ZCBCB 102   **Rel:** Feb 1973[2]   **RRP:** £1.49[2]
8–track: Y8BCB 102   **Rel:** Feb 1973[2]   **RRP:** £1.49[2]

Included a B&C "19/11" price sticker on the sleeve.

BCM 103   VARIOUS ARTISTS: Battle Of The Bands

1. All By Myself (Shakin' Stevens And The Sunsets)
2. I'm Movin' On (Gene Vincent And The Houseshakers)
3. Lucille (Dave Travis And Bad River)
4. I Don't Wanna Discuss It (Carol Grimes And The Red Price Band)
5. My Babe (Lee Tracy And The Tributes)
6. Lovin' Up a Storm (Memphis Index)

1. Say Mama (Gene Vincent And The Houseshakers)
2. Odessa (Wild Angels)
3. Wee Dock And Doris (Red Price Band)
4. Right Behind You Baby (The Houseshakers)
5. Let the Good Times Roll (Merrill Moore)
6. Lotta Lovin' (Impalas)
7. I'm Walking (Rock And Roll Allstars)

Label: BC3
Rel: Apr/Jun '71[1]
RRP: 99p[1]

Inner sleeve. Shakin' Stevens comes out well on top in this mostly lacklustre battle of the bands!

BCM 104   **ROCK 'N' ROLL ALLSTARS: Red China Rocks**

1. Slippin' And A Sliding
2. Peggy Sue
3. Slow Down
4. Dixie Fried
5. Folsom Prison Blues
6. Blue Suede Shoes
7. 20 Flight Rock

1. Long Tall Sally
2. Rip It Up
3. Bonie Moronie
4. Shakin' All Over
5. It Keeps Raining
6. One Hand Loose
7. My Girl Josephine

Label: BC3
Rel: Jun/Jul '72[1]
RRP: 99p[1]

Cassette: ZCBCB 104
8–track: Y8BCB 104

Rel: Dec 1972[2]
Rel: Dec 1972[2]

RRP: £1.49[2]
RRP: £1.49[2]

BCM 105   **VARIOUS ARTISTS: Rock 'N' Roll Party**

1. My Babe (Lee Tracy)
2. Sally Anne (Wild Angels)
3. Say Mamma (Gene Vincent)
4. Sweet Mama Tree Top Tall (Merrill Moore)
5. Rip It Up (Rock And Roll Allstars)
6. Time To Kill (Wild Angels)
7. Bye Bye Love (Rock And Roll Allstars)
8. Get It On (Rock And Roll Allstars)

1. All By Myself (Shakin' Stevens)
2. I'm Moving On (Gene Vincent)
3. It's Late (Wild Angels)
4. Bonie Maronie (Rock And Roll Allstars)
5. Wrong Number Try Again (Wild Angels)
6. Let The Good Times Roll (Merrill Moore)
7. Three Nights A Week (Wild Angels)
8. It Keeps Raining (Rock And Roll Allstars)
9. Let's Work Together (Rock And Roll Allstars)

Label: BC3
Rel: Dec 1972[1]/ Jan 1973[1]
RRP: 99p[1]

CB sequence 7" singles

Charisma singles were issued on B&C's pre–existing CB catalogue number sequence. No distinction was made between the early mono and later stereo issues. The first B&C record on the CB sequence was Merrill Moore's *Sweet Mama Tree Top Tall* (CB 101), released the week of 2 May 1969, whilst the first Charisma release was Topo D. Bil's *Witchi–Tai–To* (CB 116), released the week of 23 January 1970. The last B&C label record was Jawbone's *Gotta Go* (CB 190) in August 1972. From this point onward the sequence was used exclusively by Charisma until 1987, when that label was absorbed into Virgin.

CB 100   **MERRILL MOORE: Sweet Mama Tree Top Tall / Little Green Apples**
Label: BC1   **Rel:** 2 May 1969[3]

CB 101   **JAMES CARR: Freedom Train / That's The Way Love Turned Out For Me**
Label: BC1   **Rel:** 2 May 1969[3]
Promotional copies exist with "D.J. copy not for resale" on the label.

CB 102   **BOB AND EARL: Dancin' Everywhere / Baby It's Over**
Label: BC1   **Rel:** 16 May or 23 May 1969[3]

CB 103   **THE KENTUCKIANS: Pop–A–Top / How'd We Ever Get This Way**
Label: BC1   **Rel:** 13 Jun or 20th Jun 1969[3]

CB 104   **HORACE FAITH: Spinning Wheel / Like I Used To Do**
Label: BC1   **Rel:** 13 Jun or 20 Jun 1969[3]

The B&C Discography: 1968 to 1975

CB 105   **JACKIE LEE AND DELORES HALL: Whether It's Right Or Wrong / Baby I'm Satisfied**
Label: BC2   **Rel:** 25 Jul or 1 Aug 1969[3]
Originally intended for issue on the Action label ("ACT+4544+A"/"ACT+4544+B" crossed out in the run–off). Promotional copies with large "A" on label. Jackie Lee was a pseudonym for Earl Nelson, of Bob and Earl. *Baby I'm Satisfied* originally issued on Sue (WI 393) in 1965, credited to Bob and Earl.

CB 106   **CLYDE McPHATTER: Denver / Tell Me**
Label: BC2   **Rel:** 6 Oct 1969[3]

CB 107   **AARON NEVILLE: Tell It Like It Is / Why Worry**
Label: BC2   **Rel:** 22 Aug 1969[3]
Originally issued on Stateside as SS 584 in 1967. *Record Retailer* has a release date of 8 Aug.

CB 108   **NO RELEASE**
The B&C/Action/Stable catalogue for 1970 confirms no release on this catalogue number. In 1980 a pirate David Bowie single in picture sleeve (*The Ching–A–Ling Song / Supermen*) appeared on this catalogue number but with a very unconvincing B&C label design.

CB 109   **NO RELEASE**
The B&C/Action/Stable catalogue for 1970 confirms no release on this catalogue number.

CB 110   **DON FOX: Once In A While / You Belong To My Heart**
Label: BC2   **Rel:** 3 Oct 1969[3]

CB 111   **SIMON K: You Know I Do / Bring Your Love Back**
Label: BC2   **Rel:** 5 Dec 1969[3]

CB 112   **THE HOUSE OF LORDS: In The Land Of Dreams / Ain't Gonna Wait Forever**
Label: BC2   **Rel:** 24 Oct 1969[3]

CB 113   **GINGERBREAD: How Are You / Easy Girl**
Label: BC2   **Rel:** 31 Oct 1969[3]
DJ copies exist with "DJ COPY" and small "A" on the label.

CB 114   **WILD ANGELS: Buzz Buzz / Please Don't Touch**
Label: BC2   **Rel:** 21 Nov 1969[3]

CB 115   **DRY ICE: Running To The Convent / Nowhere To Go**
Label: BC2   **Rel:** 5 Dec 1969[3]

CB 116   **TOPO D. BIL: Witchi–Tai–To / Jam (Charisma)**
Label: CH1   **Rel:** 23 Jan 1970[3]
Picture sleeve. Some picture sleeves include an incorrect "CB 114" catalogue number with misspelled track credit, "Wichi–Tai–To" (i.e. missing out the "t" in the first word).

CB 117   **JILL DAY: I'll Think About You / The Way of Love**
Label: BC2   **Rel:** 1 May 1970[3]

CB 118   **RICHARD TURNER: Serenade To Summertime / Starshine (NOT RELEASED)**

CB 118   **THE JOHNNY ARTHEY ORCHESTRA: Serenade To The Summer / Star Shine**

Label: BC2   **Rel:** 6 Mar 1970[3]

First listed in *The New Singles* for 13 February 1970 credited to Richard Turner, whoever he was – perhaps the backing track sounded better without the singer and they wiped the vocal track. Who knows? The March notification in *The New Singles* (i.e. the released version) credits the titles as per the February listing (though now with correct artist). Picture sleeve credits b–side as "Star's Shine".

CB 119   **THE FORUM: The River Is Wide / I Fall In Love All Over Again**
Label: BC2   **Rel:** 6 Feb 1970[3]
Originally issued on London as HLM 10120 in 1967.

CB 120   **RARE BIRD: Sympathy / Devil's High Concern (Charisma)**
Label: CH1   **Rel:** 6 Feb 1970[3]
Deleted: 1973 (MMSC3)
Most copies are Orlake pressings, though three–pronged Philips–pressed copies are also confirmed.

CB 121   **ATOMIC ROOSTER: Friday The Thirteenth / Banstead**
Label: BC1   **Rel:** 13 Mar 1970[3]
Picture sleeve credits "Friday the 13th" whilst label credits "Friday the Thirteenth".

CB 122   **VAN DER GRAAF GENERATOR: Refugees / Boat Of A Million Years (Charisma)**
Label: CH1   **Rel:** 17 Apr 1970[3]
All known copies are three–prong Philips pressings. The a–side is a different version to that on *The Least We Can Do Is Wave To Each Other* (CAS 1007) and feels very similar to the original LP mix

---

CB 123   **WILD ANGELS: Sally Ann / Wrong Number, Try Again**
Label: BC2   **Rel:** 5 Jun 1970[3]

CB 124   **BENNETT AND EVANS: No, No You Don't Know / The Path Is Hard To Follow**
Label: BC2   **Rel:** 26 Jun 1970[3]

CB 125   **FREDDIE NOTES AND THE RUDIES: It Came Out Of The Sky / Well Oh Well**
Label: BC2   **Rel:** 17 Apr 1970[3]
Picture sleeve.

CB 126   **AUDIENCE: Belladonna Moonshine / The Big Spell (Charisma)**
Label: CH1   **Rel:** 26 Jun 1970[3]
Solid–centred Orlake pressings and Philips pressings with large centre–hole exist.

CB 127   **SWEET SALVATION: Honey Man / Freedom City**
Label: BC2   **Rel:** 10 Jul 1970[3]
A–side reissued in Jan 1971 on CB 139 with new b–side. *Honey Man* was co–composed by Cat Stevens and was supposedly to be recorded with Elton John, though this plan fell through.

CB 128   **RAY MORGAN: Long And Winding Road / The Sweetest Wine**
Label: BC2   **Rel:** 3 Jul 1970[3]/19 Oct 1973[3]
Obviously plenty of copies still in stock at B&C's warehouse in 1973!

CB 129   **CAROL GRIMES AND DELIVERY: Harry Lucky / Homemade Ruin**
Label: BC2   **Rel:** 28 Aug 1970[3]
Probably the first single pressing under the contract with EMI.

The B&C Discography: 1968 to 1975

CB 130   TREVOR BILLMUSS: Whoops Amour / Sunday Afternoon In Belgrave Square (Charisma)
Label: CH1   **Rel:** 25 Sep 1970[3]

CB 131   ATOMIC ROOSTER: Tomorrow Night / Play The Game
Label: BC2   **Rel:** 25 Sep 1970[3]
White label test pressings exist.

CB 132   THE NICE: Country Pie / One Of Those People (Charisma)
Label: CH1   **Rel:** 6 Nov 1970[3]

CB 133   FRIENDSHIP: The World Is Going To Be A Better Place / A Million Hearts
Label: BC2   **Rel:** 6 Nov 1970[3]

CB 134   LEWIS RICH: The Prophet / Freedom City
Label: BC2   **Rel:** 20 Nov 1970[3]
Promotional copies came in a picture sleeve with the following text, "The record sleeve of "The Prophet" is promotional only and will not be used in the general distribution to the record." All well and good, except the record was issued in a picture sleeve that was exactly the same except that it did not include the above text. The exact truth is often misleading.

CB 135   RAY MORGAN: Barefoot Days / Love Doesn't Change
Label: BC2   **Rel:** 20 Nov 1970[3]

CB 136   SWEET SALVATION: Honey Man / Crucifix, Swastika And Star
Label: BC2   **Rel:** 29 Jan or 5 Feb 1971[3]
A–side previously issued on CB 127 with different b–side.

CB 137   LINDISFARNE: Clear White Light – Part 2 / Knacker's Yard Blues (Charisma)
Label: CH1   **Rel:** 20 Nov 1970[3]

CB 138   RARE BIRD: What You Want To Know / Hammerhead (Charisma)
Label: CH1   **Rel:** 27 Nov 1970[3]
A–side seems to be a remixed version of the album track from CAS 1011 with more prominent cymbals – though perhaps this is just something to do with re–cutting for single.

CB 139   THE WEATHERMEN: It's The Same Old Song / Why Should I Fight
Label: BC2   **Rel:** 11 Dec 1970[3]

CB 140   RAY MORGAN: No More Tears / Wheel Keeps Turning
Label: BC2   **Rel:** 29 Jan or 5 Feb 1971[3]

CB 141   AUDIENCE: Indian Summer / It Brings A Tear (DJ COPY)
CB 141   AUDIENCE: Indian Summer / It Brings A Tear / Priestess
Label: CH2   **Rel:** 19 Feb[8]/26 Mar 1971[3]
Picture sleeve. Different (and better) version of *Priestess* to that on the album. Version as released includes two tracks on a–side. The two track DJ version (*Indian Summer* b/w *It Brings a Tear*) includes February release date and matrix numbers ("CB. 141A/2U"/"CB. 141A/3U") on labels. So both this and the following Audience single ended up with amended tracks and delayed release.

CB 142   REDWOOD: Didn't I (Blow Your Mind) / Homemade Happy Day
Label: BC2   **Rel:** 12 Feb 1971[3]
Exists with both solid and 4–prong die–cut centres.

The B&C Discography: 1968 to 1975

CB 143	*NO RELEASE*	

CB 144	*NO RELEASE*	

CB 145   **WILD ANGELS: Three Nights A Week / Time To Kill**
Label: BC2   Rel: 2 Apr 1971[3]

CB 146   **EVERYONE: Trouble At The Mill / Radio Lady**
Label: BC2   Rel: 2 Apr 1971[3]

CB 147   **THE WEATHERMEN: Honey Bee (Keep On Stinging Me) / Anarchy Rock)**
Label: BC2   Rel: 9 Apr 1971[3]

CB 148   **EMPEROR ROSKO: Customs Man / Take It In Your Stride**
Label: BC2   Rel: 16 Apr 1971[3]

CB 149   **THE ARNOLD CORNS: Moonage Daydream / Hang On To Yourself**
Label: BC2   Rel: 23 Apr 1971[3]

CB 150   **RAY MORGAN: Let's Fall In Love Again / The Path Is Hard To Follow**
Label: BC2   Rel: 21 May 1971[3]

CB 151   **BITCH: Laughing / House Where I Live**
Label: BC2   Rel: 21 May[3]/11 Jun 1971[3]
The New Singles for 11 June miscredits the band as "Hitch".

CB 152   **GENESIS: The Knife / The Knife (Part 2) (Charisma)**
Label: CH2   Rel: 21 May 1971[3]
Picture sleeve shows the then new line–up with Phil Collins and Steve Hackett although John Mayhew and Anthony Phillips play on the record.

CB 153   **LINDISFARNE: Lady Eleanor / Nothing But The Marvellous Is Beautiful (Charisma)**
Label: CH2   Rel: 21 May 1971[3]
A2U/B2U matrix copies exist with credit "From the L.P. CAS 1025 – "Nicely Out Of Tune"" on the a–side label (four prong die–cut and solid centred copies have credit). However, some A2U/B2U copies as well as A3U/B2U copies exist without the LP credit. A1U/B1U and A3U/B2U matrix copies are confirmed in picture sleeve. There are two different versions ("Music playing in my bone" as opposed to "Music playing in my bones") – sorry, haven't got a clue which matrix is which version! Original handwritten lyrics by Alan Hull titled "Lady Elenore (Nightmare Festival)".

CB 154   **THE HERD: You've Got Me Hanging From Your Lovin' Tree / I Don't Wanna Go To Sleep Again**
Label: BC2   Rel: 4 Jun 1971[3]

CB 155   **ROCK AND ROLL ALLSTARS: Baby Can You Feel It / It Keeps Raining**
Label: BC2   Rel: 28 May[3]/18 Jun 1971[3]

The B&C Discography: 1968 to 1975

CB 156 AUDIENCE: Raviole / Eye To Eye (NOT RELEASED)
CB 156 AUDIENCE: Eye To Eye / Eye To Eye (MISPRESS? PROMO?)
CB 156 AUDIENCE: You're Not Smiling / Eye To Eye
Label: CH2   Rel: 16 Jul 1971[3] (as released)
The New Singles lists "Raviole" for release on 28 May 1971. Why this coupling was pulled from release is unknown – do test pressings exist? Copies then appeared, for no adequately explored reason, with the b–side on both sides. Next up was a promotional pressing (BCP 1) with changed a–side. Almost two months after first notification CB 156 appeared in the shops with tracks as per BCP 1. Oddly, some stock copies exist with a very large "A" hand stamped on the b–side.

CB 157 ATOMIC ROOSTER: Devil's Answer / The Rock
Label: BC2   Rel: 28 May 1971[3]
A 7" pressing on a 12" acetate plate exists with credits written in what looks like chalk.

CB 158 TREVOR BILLMUSS: English Pastures / Fishing Songs
Label: BC2   Rel: 18 Jun 1971[3]
The b–side is taken from the Charisma LP (CAS 1017), where it is titled "Fishing Song".

CB 159 GARY CHARLES: You've Been Away Too Long / Lovely Linda
Label: BC2   Rel: 16 Jul 1971[3]

CB 160 JO TAYLOR: The Junkman's Serenade / You Fooled Me
Label: BC2   Rel: 30 Jul 1971[3]

CB 161 MARC ELLINGTON: Alligator Man / Song For A Friend
Label: BC2   Rel: 30 Jul 1971[3]

CB 162 THE WEATHERMEN: Fine Together Stomp / Fred Parsons, Jim Flynn, Waxie Maxie, Lee Gopthal, Old Uncle Clive Crawley And All
Label: BC2   Rel: 27 Aug 1971[3]

CB 163 FRIENDSHIP: Stop Living Alone / Friends Make Living What It Is
Label: BC2   Rel: 24 Sep 1971[3]

CB 164 STEELEYE SPAN: Rave On / Reels / Female Drummer
Label: BC2   Rel: 1 Oct 1971[3]
Picture sleeve.

CB 165 PAUL KENT: Do You / Helpless Harry
Label: BC2   Rel: 29 Oct 1971[3]

CB 166 MOTHER NATURE: Orange Days And Purple Nights / Where Did She Go
Label: BC2   Rel: 1 Oct[3]/5th Nov 1971[3]

CB 167 RAY MORGAN: Friend, Lover, Woman, Wife / Burning Bridges
Label: BC2   Rel: 5 Nov 1971[3]

CB 168 JAW BONE JUG BAND: Jailhouse Rock / Jugband Music
Label: BC2   Rel: 19 Nov 1971[3]

CB 169 WISHFUL THINKING: Lu La Le Lu / We're Gonna Change All This
Label: BC2   Rel: 4 Feb 1972[3]

The B&C Discography: 1968 to 1975

CB 170 **BELL AND ARC:** She Belongs To Me / Dawn (Charisma)
Label: CH2 **Rel:** 3 Dec 1971[3]

CB 171 **ROCK AND ROLL ALLSTARS:** Rock And Roll Allstars Play Party Rock: Boney Moroney/Get It On/Rip It Up / Rock And Roll Allstars Play Party Rock: Let's Work Together/It Keeps Raining/Bye Bye Love
Label: BC2 **Rel:** 17 Dec 1971[3]
Medleys with dubbed applause. Mistakenly listed in *The New Records* with LP list price of £2.05.

CB 172 **JIMMY JUSTICE:** English Rose / Burgandy, Port And Red Wine
Label: BC2 **Rel:** 7th Jan[8]/21 Jan 1972[3]
Promotional copies with 4-prong centre exist.

CB 173 **LINDISFARNE:** Meet Me On The Corner / Scotch Mist / No Time To Lose (Charisma)
Label: CH2 **Rel:** 14 Jan[3]/11 Feb 1972[3]
Issued in two different picture sleeves: original sleeve advertises only *Fog on the Tyne* (CAS 1050) on the reverse, whilst the later sleeve also advertises *Nicely out of Tune* (CAS 1025).

CB 174 **GARY CHARLES:** Love Into My Life / When You Run Out Of Breath
Label: BC2 **Rel:** 11 Feb 1972[3]

CB 175 **VAN DER GRAAF GENERATOR:** Theme One / W (Charisma)
Label: CH2 **Rel:** 4 Feb 1972[3]
Solid centre copies with picture sleeve confirmed. Whether 4-prong copies were also issued with picture sleeve is unknown. Has "BCP 6" crossed out in the run-off.

CB 176 **NEW YORK PUBLIC LIBRARY:** Whei Ling Ty Luu / Boozy Queen
Label: BC2 **Rel:** 25th Feb[8]/17 Mar 1972[3]
Promotional copies with 4-prong centres exist.

CB 177 **FICKLE PICKLE:** American Pie / Blown Away
Label: BC2 **Rel:** 21 Jan 1972[3]

CB 178 **FICKLE PICKLE:** California Calling / Doctor Octopus
Label: BC2 **Rel:** 3 Mar 1972[3]

CB 179 **RARE BIRD:** Sympathy / Devil's High Concern / What You Want To Know / Hammerhead (Charisma)
Label: CH2 **Rel:** 28 Apr 1972[3]
Solid centre copies with picture sleeve confirmed. Whether 4-prong copies were also issued with picture sleeve is unknown.

CB 180 **MARTYN KAYE:** Changes / Bad Bad Jo-Jo
Label: BC2 **Rel:** 21 Apr 1972[3/8]

CB 181 **GENESIS:** Happy The Man / Seven Stones (Charisma)
Label: CH2 **Rel:** 12 May 1972[3]
Promotional and early stock copies have 4-prong centres. Promotional copies have "DJ sample, not for resale" text on the label. If you bought this on the day of release, then you didn't get a picture sleeve. If you left it a couple of weeks, then you got the picture sleeve. Not fair, eh?

CB 182　　COMBINED SUPPORTERS CLUB: *We Are The Champions, Part 1 /*
　　　　　　　　We Are The Champions, Part 2 (Sing–Along Version)
Label: BC2　　　　Rel: 21 Apr 1972[3]

CB 183　　SPREADEAGLE: *Scipio (Charisma) (NOT RELEASED)*
CB 183　　SPREADEAGLE: *How Can We Be Lost / Nightmare (Charisma)*
Label: CH2　　　　Rel: 26 May[3]/9 Jun 1972[8]
Promotional copies with 4–prong centre confirmed and normal picture sleeve copies with solid label confirmed. A different release might have been planned for this catalogue number – the promotional single, BCP 7, has "CB 183 A – 1U" scratched out in the run-off on the Spreadeagle side.

CB 184　　WISHFUL THINKING: *Clear White Light / Hiroshima*
Label: BC2　　　　Rel: 5 May 1972[3]
Exists with both solid and 4–prong centres.

CB 185　　AUDIENCE: *Stand By The Door / Thunder And*
　　　　　　　　Lightning (Charisma)
Label: CH2　　　　Rel: 30 Jun 1972[3]

CB 186　　RAY MORGAN: *Let's Go Where The Good Times Go / San Diego*
Label: BC2　　　　Rel: 2 Jun 1972[3]

CB 187　　A. AND A. NORTH: *Rosemary / Travelling Band*
Label: BC2　　　　Rel: 28 Jul 1972[3]

CB 188　　THE JOHNNY ARTHEY ORCHESTRA: *Serenade To Summer /*
　　　　　　　　Star Shine
Label: BC2　　　　Rel: 16 Jun 1972[3]
Reissue of CB 118, though not in picture sleeve this time around.

CB 189　　ARNOLD CORNS: *Hang On To Yourself / Man In The Middle*
Label: BC2　　　　Rel: 25 Aug 1972[3]
By this time Bowie was a star, but the reissue of the previous b–side (CB 149) as an a–side failed to arouse much interest. Reissued on Mooncrest as MOON 25 the week starting 17 May 1974[3]. All three B&C–era tracks appeared on a pirate EP in 1978, complete with a creditable imitation of the B&C label and a CB 200 catalogue number, even though this number had been used by Charisma.

CB 190　　JAWBONE: *Gotta Go / Automobile Blues*
Label: BC2　　　　Rel: 25 Aug 1972[3/8]
From this point onwards the CB catalogue sequence was used exclusively by Charisma. See the sister volume to this discography, *The Famous Charisma Discography*, for further B&C–era Charisma label CB sequence singles.

Promotional 7" singles

The BCP sequence is very frustrating with many numbers still unaccounted for. Some may not have been used, or may have been used for just a handful of test pressings. Added to this is the fact that B&C used the sequence across various labels – see the relevant sections in the Action, Pegasus/Peg and People discographies for BCP records on those labels – so it is possible that missing numbers might have been used with other B&C–related labels, such as Trojan or any of that label's many subsidiary labels. It may take years for information about missing numbers to appear, if it ever does. In the meantime, it might be worth checking any B&C or related label for crossed out BCP matrix numbers – that's how the identity of BCP 6 came about!

The B&C Discography: 1968 to 1975

CB sequence DJ copy with track discrepency

CB 141   **AUDIENCE: Indian Summer / It Brings A Tear (DJ COPY)**
The two track DJ version includes a 19 February 1970 release date and matrix numbers ("CB. 141A/2U"/"CB. 141A/3U") on labels. The single as later released (in March) had both these tracks on the a–side and had a different version of *Priestess* to that included on the LP (CAS 1012) as b–side

Custom catalogue numbers

JH 1/JH 2   **JACKSON HEIGHTS: Doubting Thomas / Insomnia (Charisma)**
Promotional–only single for the the Charisma LP, *King Progress* LP (CAS 1018). Labels are marked "Promotional Copy" and "Not For Resale". The a–side has "JH 1" as the catalogue number, whilst b–side has "JH 2".

GS 1/GS 2   **GENESIS: Looking For Someone / Visions Of Angels (Charisma)**
Promotional–only single for the Charisma LP, *Trespass* (CAS 1020). The a–side has "GS 1" as the catalogue number, whilst the b–side has "GS 2".

BD 1/BD 2   **EVERY WHICH WAY: Go Placidly / The Light (Charisma)**
Promotional–only single for the Charisma LP, *Every Which Way* (CAS 1021). The a–side has "BD 1" as the catalogue number, whilst the b–side has "BD 2". Labels credit "Brian Davison's Every Witch Way", complete with the misspelling of "Which".

HB 1/HB 2   **HANNIBAL: Winds Of Change / Winter**
Promotional–only single for the B&C LP, Hannibal (CAS 1022). A–side has "HB 1" as the catalogue number and b–side has "HB 2".

BCP sequence

BCP 1   **AUDIENCE: Your Not Smiling / Eye To Eye**
Wraparound picture sleeve. A–side spelled as above – the normal issue on CB 156 was corrected to read "You're Not Smiling".

BCP 2   **CAROL GRIMES: I Don't Wanna Discuss It / ROCK AND ROLL ALLSTARS: I'm Walking**
Both tracks are from the B&C various artists LP, *Battle of the Bands Vol. 1* (BCM 103). On the LP, the a–side is credited to "Carol Grimes & the Red River Band". Is this version credired to Grimes alone?

BCP 6   **VAN DER GRAAF GENERATOR: Theme One / W (Charisma)**
Normal stock copies (CB 175) have "BCP 6" crossed out in the run–off. This does not seem to have been pressed on the promotional catalogue number (or, at least, no copy has yet come to light in collectors' circles). White label test pressings may turn up with only the BCP matrix.

BCP 7   **SPREADEAGLE: Nightingale Lane [plays Scipio, see below]/ CAPABILITY BROWN: Liar (Charisma)**
Picture sleeve with what looks like a Terry Gilliam design. The Spreadeagle track is actually *Scipio* and not *Nightingale Lane* as stated – a B&C/Charisma promotional sheet sent out with the record pointed this out. The labels are marked "For Promotion Only – Not For Sale". Issued to promote Spreadeagle's *The Piece of Paper* (CAS 1055) and Capability Brown's *From Scratch* (CAS 1056) LPs. Oddly, the Spreadeagle side has "CB 183 A–1U" scratched out in the run–off groove (CB 183 was issued with Spreadeagle's *How Can We Be Lost* and *Nightmare*).

BCP 9   **CAPABILITY BROWN: Liar (Charisma)**
One–sided copy exists with hand–written white label. This looks to have been pressed up in advance of *Liar* being issued as a single in its own right on CB 217.

Pegasus and Peg

PEG sequence LPs

PEG 1 **ATOMIC ROOSTER: In Hearing Of**

1. Breakthrough	1. Black Snake	**Label**: PE1
2. Break The Ice	2. Head In The Sky	**Rel**: pres. Aug '71
3. Decision/Indecision	3. The Rock	
4. A Spoonful Of Bromide Helps The Pulse Rate Go Down	4. The Price	

Cassette: ZCPEG 1	**Rel**: Apr 1972[2]	**RRP**: £2.50[2]
8-track: Y8PEG 1	**Rel**: Apr 1972[2]	**RRP**: £2.60[2]

PEG 2 **RICOTTI AND ALBUQUERQUE: First Wind**

1. Ratsa (Don't Know Why)	1. Bobo's Party	**Label**: PE1
2. Lo And Behold	2. Didn't Wanna Have To Do It	**Rel**: pres. Aug '71
3. Go Out And Get It	3. Old Ben Houston	
4. Don't You Believe Me?	4. The Wind Has No Love	
5. New York Windy Day	5. Give A Damn	

Trivia: Melanie's surname is miscredited on the sleeve as "Satka", though the label gets it right.

PEG 3 **THREE MAN ARMY: Third Of A Lifetime**

1. Butter Queen	1. Three Man Army	**Label**: PE1
2. Daze	2. Agent Man	**Rel**: pres. Aug '71
3. Another Day	3. See What I Took	
4. A Third Of A Lifetime	4. Midnight	
5. Nice One	5. Together	

PEG 4 **BIG SLEEP: Bluebell Wood**

1. Death Of A Hope	1. Bluebell Wood	**Label**: PE1
2. Odd Song	2. Watching Love Grow	**Rel**: pres. Aug '71
3. Free Life	3. When The Sun Was Out	
4. Aunty James		
5. Saint And Sceptic		

PEG 5 **ANDY ROBERTS: Nina And The Dream Tree**

1. Keep My Children Warm	1. Good Time Charlie	**Label**: PE1
2. I've Seen The Movie	2. Dream Tree Sequence	**Rel**: Oct 1971[1]
3. 25 Hours A Day/Breakdown/ Welcome Home		**RRP**: £2.19½[1]

Cassette: ZCPEG 5	**Rel**: Jul 1972[2]	**RRP**: £2.25[2]
8-track: Y8PEG 5	**Rel**: Jul 1972[2]	**RRP**: £2.35[2]

Sleeve (though not label) includes subcredits "Aslaug's Song" and "Nina's Song" for track 2, side 2.

PEG 6 **MARTIN CARTHY AND DAVE SWARBRICK: Selections**

1. The Man of Burnham Town	1. The Banks	**Label**: PE1
2. Creeping Jane	2. The Bloody Gardener	**Rel**: Oct 1971[1]
3. The Irish Waterwoman/The Ash Plant	3. Grey Daylight/Jenny's Chickens	**RRP**: £2.19½[1]
	4. Gentleman Soldier	
4. Lucy Wan	5. Long Lankin	
5. Matt Hyland	6. Davy Lowston	
6. The Wife Of The Soldier		

The B&C Discography: 1968 to 1975

Cassette: ZCPEG 6   **Rel:** Jul 1972[2]   **RRP:** £2.25[2]
8–track: Y8PEG 6   **Rel:** Jul 1972[2]   **RRP:** £2.35[2]
"CAS 1046" crossed out in the run–off.

PEG 7   SHIRLEY COLLINS AND THE ALBION COUNTRY BAND: No Roses

1. Claudy Banks
2. The Little Gypsy Girl
3. Banks Of The Bann
4. Murder Of Maria Marten

1. Van Dieman's Land
2. Just As The Tide Was Flowing
3. The White Hare
4. Hal–An–Tow
5. Poor Murdrered Woman

Label: PE1
Rel: Oct 1971[1]
RRP: £2.19½[1]

Cassette: ZCPEG 7   **Rel:** Jul 1972[2]   **RRP:** £2.25[2]
8–track: Y8PEG 7   **Rel:** Jul 1972[2] (del: 1977[5])   **RRP:** £2.35[2]
"CAS 1047" crossed out in the run–off. Confirmed on both Pegasus and Peg labels.

PEG 8   FUCHSIA: Fuchsia

1. Gone With The Mouse
2. A Tiny Book
3. Another Nail

1. Shoes And Ships
2. The Nothing Song
3. Me And My Kite
4. Just Anyone

Label: PE1
Rel: Oct 1971[1]
RRP: £2.19½[1]

PEG 9   STEELEYE SPAN: Ten Man Mop, Or Mr. Reservoir Butler Rides Again

1. Gower Wassail
2. Jigs: Paddy Clancey's Jig/
    Willie Clancy's Fancy
3. Four Nights Drunk
4. When I Was On Horseback

1. Marrowbones
2. Captain Coulston
3. Reels: Dowd's Favourite/£10 Float/
    The Morning Dew
4. Wee Weaver
5. Skewball

Label: PE1
Rel: Nov 1971[1]
RRP: £2.19½[1]

Cassette: ZCPEG 9   **Rel:** Apr 1972[2]   **RRP:** £2.50[2]
8–track: Y8PEG 9   **Rel:** Apr 1972[2]   **RRP:** £2.60[2]
Embossed sleeve. Inner sleeve and 8–page booklet.

PEG 10   NAZARETH: Nazareth

1. Witchdoctor Woman
2. Dear John
3. Empty Arms, Empty Heart
4. I Had A Dream
5. Red Light Lady

1. Fat Man
2. Country Girl
3. Morning Dew
4. The King Is Dead

Label: PE1
Rel: Nov 1971[1]
RRP: £2.19½[1]

Cassette: ZCPEG 10   **Rel:** Sep 1972[2]   **RRP:** £2.35[2]
8–track: Y8PEG 10   **Rel:** Sep 1972[2]   **RRP:** £2.35[2]
Matt sleeve (later Peg copies in glossy sleeve). Track 5, side 1 subtitled "(parts 1 & 2)" on sleeve but not label. There seems to be a mismatch in release dates between tape and LP versions.

PEG 11   RITCHIE FRANCIS: Songbird

1, Song Bird
2. Dizzy Sycamore
3. I'm Not Alone
4. It Will Last
5. My Music

1. Don't You Ask Me Why
2. There's A Time
3. Yet To Come
4. Friends
5. You're Never Gonna Make It
6. To Follow You

Label: PE2
Rel: Mar 1972[1]
RRP: £2.19[1]

Cassette: ZCPEG 11   **Rel:** Apr 1972[2]   **RRP:** £2.50[2]
8–track: Y8PEG 11   **Rel:** Apr 1972[2]   **RRP:** £2.60[2]
The "Pegasus" credit on sleeve amended to read "Peg". First Peg label LP, presumably.

The B&C Discography: 1968 to 1975

PEG 12   MARTIN CARTHY: Shearwater

1. I Was A Young Man
2. Banks Of Green Willow
3. Handsome Polly–O
4. Outlandish Knight
5. He Called For A Candle

1. John Blunt
2. Lord Randall
3. William Taylor
4. Famous Flower Of Serving Men
5. Betsy Bell And Mary Gray

Label: PE2
Rel: Mar 1972[1]
RRP: £2.19[1]

Cassette: ZCPEG 12
8–track: Y8PEG 12
Insert.

Rel: Apr 1972[2]
Rel: Apr 1972[2] (del: 1977[5])

RRP: £2.50[2]
RRP: £2.60[2]

PEG 13   SPIROGYRA: Old Boot Wine

1. Dangerous Dave
2. Van Allen's Belt
3. Runaway
4. Grandad
5. Wings of Thunder

1. World's Eyes
2. Don't Let It Get You
3. Disraeli's Problem
4. A Canterbury Tale

Label: PE2
Rel: Jun 1972[1]
RRP: £2.08[1]

Cassette: ZCPEG 13
8–track: Y8PEG 13

Rel: Jun 1972[2]
Rel: Jun 1972[2]

RRP: £2.25[2]
RRP: £2.35[2]

PEG 14   NAZARETH: Exercises

1. I Will Not Be Led
2. Cat's Eye, Apple Pie
3. In My Time
4. Woke Up This Morning
5. Called Her Name

1. Fool About You
2. Love Now Your Gone
3. Madelaine
4. Sad Song
5. 1692 (Glen Coe Massacre)

Label: PE2
Rel: Jun 1972[1]
RRP: £2.08[1]

Cassette: ZCPEG 14
8–track: Y8PEG 14

Rel: Aug 1972[2]
Rel: Aug 1972[2]

RRP: £2.25[2]
RRP: £2.35[2]

Track listing from labels. Sleeve credits track 2, side 2 as "Love, Now You're Gone".

PS sequence LPs

PS 1   VARIOUS ARTISTS: Clogs

1. Captain Coulston (Steeleye Span)
2. Richmond (Andy Roberts)
3. The Irish Waterwoman/The Ash Plant (Martin Carthy And Dave Swarbrick)
4. The King (Steeleye Span)
5. Poem (Keith Christmas)
6. Murder Of Maria Maren (Shirley Collins)

1. Rave On (Steeleye Span)
2. I Live Not Where I Love (Tim Hart And Maddy Prior)
3. Captain's Log (Spirogira)
4. Rod's Song (Shelagh McDonald)
5. Lord Randall (Martin Carthy)
6. Yarrow (Marc Ellington)
7. Welcome Home (Andy Roberts)

Label: PE2
Rel: Apr 1972[1]
RRP: 99p[1]

Cassette: ZCPS 1
8–track: Y8PS 1

Rel: Jul 1972[2]
Rel: Jul 1972[2]

RRP: £1.35[2]
RRP: £1.59[2]

Subtitled "Folk Sampler". Insert. "99p" price sticker on sleeve. *Richmond* otherwise unavailable.

PS 2   VARIOUS ARTISTS: Club Folk Volume 1

1. The Sailor (Robin Scott)
2. Red And Green Christmas (Nadia Cattouse)
3. Blue Railway Fields (P C Kent)
4. The Barley Straw (Martin Carthy And Dave Swarbrick)
5. Autumn to May (Andy Roberts)
6. Travelling Down (Keith Christmas)

1. Rolling And Tumbling (Synanthesia)
2. Sweet Sunlight (Shelagh McDonald)
3. Our Captain Cried All Hands (Martin Carthy And Dave Swarbrick)
4. Come Join My Orchestra (Al Jones)
5. Disbelief Blues (Mike Hart)
6. Jello (Andy Roberts)

Label: PE2
Rel: Jul 1972[1]
RRP: 99p[1]

Textured sleeve. July edition of *The New Albums* credits PS 2 and PS 3 as "This Is Folk Vol 1" and "This Is Folk Vol 2", both with incorrect price of £2.08. August edition lists correct titles and correct price of 99p.

PS 3   **VARIOUS ARTISTS: Club Folk Volume 2**

1. Rainy Night Blues (Shelagh McDonald)
2. What I Was Thinking (Al Jones)
3. Trafalgar Square (Synanthesia)
4. Broadened (P. C. Kent)
5. The Sound Of Rain (Robin Scott)
6. B.C. People (Nadia Cattouse)

1. Domeama (Martin Carthy)
2. Where the Soul Of Man Never Dies (Andy Roberts)
3. All Around My Grandmother's Floor (Nadia Cattouse)
4. Bed–Sit Two Step (Keith Christmas)
5. Yawny Morning Song (Mike Hart)
6. Ire And Spottiswoad (Al Jones)

Label: PE2
Rel: Jul 1972[1]
RRP: 99p[1]

Textured sleeve. Miscredited in the July edition of *The New Albums* – see PS 2 above.

Tape versions of CAS sequence LPs

By the time that B&C released tape versions of LPs on the CAS sequence, the B&C label had been superceded by Pegasus, followed by Peg. Therefore, tape issues were rebranded as Peg issues, though they otherwise kept their CAS sequence numbering (e.g. CAS 1029 became ZCPEG 1029 on cassette and Y8PEG 1029 on 8–track).

ZCPEG 1029 / Y8PEG 1029   **STEELEYE SPAN: Please To See The King**
Rel: Jul 1972[2] (both formats)   **RRP:** £2.25[2] (cassette)/£2.35[2] (8–track)

ZCPEG 1035 / Y8PEG 1035   **TIM HART AND MADDY PRIOR: Summer Solstice**
Rel: Jul 1972[2] (both formats)   **RRP:** £2.25[2] (cassette)/£2.35[2] (8–track)

ZCPEG 1045 / Y8PEG 1045   **HAROLD McNAIR: Harold McNair**
Rel: May 1972[2] (both formats)   **RRP:** £2.25[2] (cassette)/£2.35[2] (8–track)

PGS sequence 7" singles

PGS 1   **THREE MAN ARMY: What's Your Name? / Travelin'**
Label: PE1   **Rel:** 5 Nov 1971[3]

PGS 2   **NAZARETH: Dear John / Friends**
PGS 2   **NAZARETH: Dear John / Occasional Failure**
Label: see below   **Rel:** 28 Jan 1972[3]

The New Singles for 28 Jan 1972 credits the b–side as "Occasional Failure", though on this release (PE1) the label credited the b–side as "Friends". The later Peg repress (PE2) credited the b–side as "Occasional Failure". It ought to be pointed out that *Occasional Failure* and *Friends* are the same track. It looks as though the original b–side label was a mistake.

PGS 3   **SPIROGYRA: Dangerous Dave / Captain's Log**
Label: PE2   **Rel:** 28 Apr 1972[3]
Picture sleeve. A–side is an edited version of the LP track from *Old Boot Wine* (PEG 13).

PGS 4   **NAZARETH: Morning Dew / Spinning Top**
Label: PE2   **Rel:** 7 Jul 1972[3]

PGS 5   **NAZARETH: If You See My Baby / Hard Living**
Label: PE2   **Rel:** 15 Sep 1972[3]

PGS 6   **STEELEYE SPAN:** *Jigs And Reels / Jigs And Reels*
Label: PE2   **Rel:** 29 Sep 1972[3]
A–side subcredit: "Reels: Dowd's Favourite; £10 Float; The Morning Dew" under the title; b–side subcredit: "Jigs: Bryan O'Lynn; The Hag With The Money; Paddy Clancey's Jig; Willie Clancy's Fancy".

Promotional 7" records

The flexidisc was pressed up to promote the first four LPs, though it is unknown as to where the record was distributed. The BCP sequence was used for promotional singles on several B&C labels. See the B&C/Charisma section for more information.

Custom catalogue number

SFI M–G1   **VARIOUS ARTISTS:** *untitled*

1. The Rock (Atomic Rooster)
2. New York Windy Day (Ricotti And Albuquerque)
1. Butter Queen (Three Man Army)
2. Saint And Sceptic (Big Sleep)

'Thick' vinyl flexidisc. No catalogue number, but the matrix number is "SFI M–G1", which presumably indicates a Sound for Industry pressing. The LP label design is used on both sides, though with no artist nor track credits. A very un rock 'n' roll spoken word introduction before each track. All tracks edited versions.

BCP sequence

BCP 3   **NAZARETH:** *Dear John / Witchdoctor Woman / Morning Dew*
Stamped white label and promotional insert. Two tracks on a–side.

BCP 8   **NAZARETH:** *Fool About You / Woke Up This Morning / Morning Dew*
Copies exist with hand–written white labels. Two tracks on a–side.

Mooncrest

From the start, Mooncrest seemed suspiciously similar to the old B&C label. Much like the old B&C label, Mooncrest suffered from an identity crisis with releases evincing a mix of styles from commercial reggae to hard rock, taking in folk and out–and–out pop along the way. Mooncrest also acquired a subsidiary label, Dragon, from Island in August 1973. What with Dragon showcasing Jamaican music from Byron Lee productions, why the label was licensed to Mooncrest and not to Trojan remains a mystery, though perhaps Mooncrest's account books looked rather more healthy than Trojan's at this point?

Long a mystery, though one now solved, is why Mooncrest didn't release cassette or 8–track versions of high–selling Steeleye Span and Nazareth LP reissues. The reason is that B&C still held large stocks of the original Pegasus and Peg tape versions. See the Pegasus and Peg listings for release information and known deletion dates for tape versions.

At least three releases were lost during B&C's liquidation – these were Decameron's *Beyond the Days* LP (despite adverts showing the sleeve appearing in the music press) an EP by their surf/doo–wop alter–egos, The Magnificent Mercury Brothers, and a single by The Fortunes. The listings are not concerned with later Mooncrest releases following the label's resurrection as part of the reconstituted B&C Recordings Ltd.

CREST sequence LPs

Many Mooncrest LPs previously released on B&C or Pegasus/Peg came complete in original sleeves with original labels and inserts until stocks on hand ran out. Sleeves included Mooncrest stickers over the old catalogue numbers. There are plenty of hybrids out there: a) original pre–Mooncrest LP with inserts and Mooncrest sticker over old catalogue number; b) Mooncrest LP with original inserts in original pre–Mooncrest sleeve with Mooncrest sticker over old catalogue number; c) Mooncrest LP in Mooncrest sleeve with original pre–Mooncrest inserts; d) Full Mooncrest issues with no inserts.

LPs up to (probably) CREST 21 were pressed by EMI, but from that point new LPs and further pressings of back catalogue were pressed by Lyntone, and possibly others.

Many sources are confused about original release dates because LPs reissued by the resurrected Mooncrest were given amended credits including a 1976 publication date. Subsequent repressings retained this 1976 publication credit. Original releases are easy to spot because they have the original 37 Soho Square address for B&C Records, whilst the 1976 reissues have Saga's Kensal Road address.

CREST 1   **NAZARETH: Razamanaz**

1. Razamanaz	1. Night Woman	**Rel:** Apr 1973[1]
2. Alcatraz	2. Bad, Bad Boy	**RRP:** £2.10[1]/
3. Vigilante Man	3. Sold My Soul	£2.14[4]
4. Woke Up This Morning	4. Too Bad, Too Bad	
	5. Broken Down Angel	

Cassette: ZCRES 1   **Rel:** Jul 1973[2]   **RRP:** £2.35[2]
8–track: Y8RES 1   **Rel:** Jul 1973[2]   **RRP:** £2.35[2]
Original copies include a Mooncrest inner sleeve advertising the first two LPs.

The B&C Discography: 1968 to 1975

CREST 2 **LIGHTHOUSE: Sunny Days**

1. Silver Bird
2. Sunny Days
3. You Girl
4. Beneath My Woman
5. Merlin

1. Broken Guitar Blues
2. Letter Home
3. You Give To Me
4. Lonely Places

Rel: Apr 1973[1]
RRP: £2.10[1]/
£2.14[4]

Cassette: ZCRES 2
8–track: Y8RES 2

Rel: Sep 1973[2]
Rel: Sep 1973[2]

RRP: £2.35[2]
RRP: £2.35[2]

Presumably included advertising inner. Relisted in the July 1973 edition of *The New Records* with a very inaccurate RRP of £1.49.

CREST 3 **HOTSHOTS: Snoopy V.s The Red Baron**

1. Snoopy V.s The Red Baron
2. Chatanooga Choo Choo
3. Knockin' On The Door
4. Cousin Of Mine
5. You Don't Know Like I know
6. Itsy Bitsy Teeny Weeny Yellow Polka Dot Bikini

1. Battle Of New Orleans
2. What Do You Say
3. Simple Simon Says
4. Yesterday Man
5. Roll Muddy River
6. I Hear You Knockin'

Rel: Oct 1973[1]
RRP: £2.14[1]
Del: 1975[5]

Cassette: ZCRES 3
8–track: Y8RES 3

Rel: Oct 1973[2]
Rel: Oct 1973[2]

RRP: £2.35[2]
RRP: £2.35[2]

Title as above as taken from labels and spine. The sleeve credits "Snoopy V.s Red Baron".

CREST 4 **NAZARETH: Loud 'N' Proud**

1. Go Down Fighting
2. Not Fakin' It
3. Turn On Your Receiver
4. Teenage Nervous Breakdown
5. Freewheeler

1. This Flight Tonight
2. Child In The Sun
3. The Ballad Of Hollis Brown

Rel: Nov 1973[1]
RRP: £2.14[1]

Cassette: ZCRES 4
8–track: Y8RES 4

Rel: Jan 1974[10]
Rel: Jan 1974[10]

RRP: prob. £2.45
RRP: prob. £2.45

CREST 5 **DANDY LIVINGSTONE: Conscious**

1. Black Connection
2. Let Me Tell You What's Goin' On
3. Black Star
4. Caribbean Rock
5. Glory Be Ay, Glory Be You

1. Everyday Gets A Little Bit Sweeter
2. I'm a Believer
3. Love Is About to Get Me
4. Jack, the King of the Tramps
5. Check Out Yourself

Rel: Dec 1973[1]
RRP: £2.14[4]/
£2.25[1]

Cassette: ZCRES 5
8–track: Y8RES 5
Textured sleeve.

Rel: Mar 1974[10]
Rel: Mar 1974[10]

RRP: prob. £2.45
RRP: prob. £2.45

CREST 6 **STU NUNNERY: Stu Nunnery**

1. The Isle Of Debris
2. And That's Fine With Me
3. Sally From Syracuse
4. Madelaine

1. Lady, It's Time to Go
2. Your Rise
3. Diminished Love
4. The Lady In Waiting
5. Roads

Rel: Feb 1974[4]
RRP: £2.25[4]
Del: 1975[5]

Cassette: ZCRES 6
8–track: Y8RES 6

Rel: May 1974[10]
Rel: May 1974[10]

RRP: prob. £2.45
RRP: prob. £2.45

Track 1, side 2 does not include the comma on the sleeve credits.

The B&C Discography: 1968 to 1975

CREST 7   BUDDY RICH: The Roar Of '74
1. Nuttville
2. Kilimanjaro Cookout
3. Big Mac
4. Backwoods Sideman

1. Time Check
2. Prelude To A Kiss
3. Waltz Of The Mushroom Hunters
4. Senator Sam

Rel: Apr 1974[4]
RRP: £2.25[4]
Del: 1975[5]

Cassette: ZCRES 7
8–track: Y8RES 7

Rel: May 1974[2]
Rel: May 1974[2]

RRP: £2.45[2]
RRP: £2.45[2]

CREST 8   STEELEYE SPAN: Please To See The King
Rel: Apr[4]/May 1974[1]   RRP: £2.25[1]   Del: 1976[5]
Refer to CAS 1029 for track listing. B&C copies in hessian feel sleeve were issued with Mooncrest sticker covering the B&C catalogue number and early Mooncrest copies still included the original B&C insert. Original Peg tape releases were still available.

**CREST 9   STEELEYE SPAN: Ten Man Mop, Or Mr. Reservoir Butler
                  Rides Again**
Rel: Apr[4]/May 1974[1]   RRP: £2.25[1]   Del: 1975[5]
Refer to PEG 9 for track listing. Early Mooncrest reissues came complete in gatefold sleeve and with an 8–page booklet. Later Mooncrest pressings housed in single sleeve without booklet. Original Peg tape releases were still available.

CREST 10   NAZARETH: Nazareth
Rel: Apr[4]/Jun 1974[1]   RRP: £2.25[1]
Refer to PEG 10 for track listing. Original Peg tape releases were still available.

CREST 11   SHIRLEY COLLINS AND THE ALBION COUNTRY BAND: No Roses
Rel: Apr[4]/Jun 1974[1]   RRP: £2.25[1]
Refer to PEG 7 for track listing. Early reissues came in the original Pegasus gatefold sleeve with Mooncrest sticker covering the PEG catalogue number. Original Peg tape releases were still available.

CREST 12   TIM HART AND MADDY PRIOR: Summer Solstice
Rel: Apr[4]/May 1974[1]   RRP: £2.25[1]
Refer to CAS 1035 for track listing. Reissued in original gatefold sleeve design with updated label credits. Original Peg tape releases were still available.

CREST 13   NO RELEASE

CREST 14   NAZARETH: Exercises
Rel: Apr 1974[4]   RRP: £2.25[4]
Refer to PEG 14 for track listing. Reissue still housed in gatefold sleeve. Original Peg tape releases were still available.

CREST 15   NAZARETH: Rampant
1. Silver Dollar Forger (Parts 1 & 2)
2. Glad When You're Gone
3. Loved and Lost
4. Shanghai'd in Shanghai

1. Jet Jag
2. Light My Way
3. Sunshine
4. (a) Shapes of Things (b) Space Safari

Rel: Apr[4]/May '74[1]
RRP: £2.25[1]

Cassette: ZCRES 15   Rel: May 1974[2]   RRP: £2.45[2]
8–track: Y8RES 15   Rel: May 1974[2]   RRP: £2.45[2]

Embossed sleeve. Inner sleeve, and dollar sticker insert, many of which got stuck to the rear of the sleeve because the track listing was on the sticker but not on the sleeve rear. Insert credits track 1, side 2 as "Jet Lag" (which sounds rather more likely than the title as included on the label, above). Sticker also shows track 4, side 2 as two tracks, credited as "(4a)" and "(4b)".

The B&C Discography: 1968 to 1975

CREST 16   TIM MOORE: Tim Moore
1. A Fool Like You
2. Second Avenue
3. Charmer
4. Sister Lilac
5. High Feeling

1. I Can Almost See The Light
2. Love Enough
3. Aviation Man
4. When You Close Your Eyes
5. I'll Be Your Time

Rel: May[1]/Jul '74[1]
RRP: £2.25[1]

Cassette: ZCRES 16   Rel: Jun 1974 [2]   RRP: £2.45[2]
8–track: Y8RES 16   Rel: Jun 1974 [2]   RRP: £2.45[2]

CREST 17   VARIOUS ARTISTS: Rave On
1. Rave On (Steeleye Span)
2. The Ploughboy And The Cockney (Tim Hart And Maddy Prior)
3. Western Wynde (Tim Hart And Maddy Prior)
4. Banks Of The Bann (Shirley Collins)
5. Cold Haily Windy Night (Steeleye Span)
6. Let No Man Steal Your Thyme (Shelagh McDonald)
7. Lovely On The Water (Steeleye Span)

1. Just As The Tide Was Flowing (Shirley Collins)
2. Cannily, Cannily (Tim Hart And Maddy Prior)
3. Matt Hyland (Martin Carthy)
4. Of All The Birds (Tim Hart And Maddy Prior)
5. The Bank (Martin Carthy And Dave Swarbrick)
6. Marrowbones (Steeleye Span)

Rel: Jun 1974[1]
RRP: £2.25[1]
Del: 1975[5]

Shirley Collins' tracks do not credit the Albion Country Band. Original issue has matt sleeve with artist photos on rear cover plus compilation, art direction, design and artwork credits. 1976 and later issues in gloss sleeve without artist photos or the above credits. Later pressing has a plain white spine with credits in different positions (cover illustration wraps around from front to back sleeve on original pressing). Relisted in the July 1974 edition of *The New Records* with RRP of £2.45.

CREST 18   IAN MATTHEWS: Journey's From Gospel Oak
1. Knowing The Game
2. Polly
3. Things You Gave Me
4. Mobile Blue
5. Tribute To Hank Williams

1. Met Her On A Plane
2. Bride 1945
3. Franklin Avenue
4. Do Right Woman
5. Sing Me Back Home

Rel: Aug 1974[1]
RRP: £2.25[4]/
£2.45[1]

Cassette: ZCRES 18   Rel: Sep 1974[2]   RRP: £2.40[2]
8–track: Y8RES 18   Rel: Sep 1974[2]   RRP: £2.40[2]

Journey From Gospel Oak was recorded for Vertigo in November 1972, but was rejected, which led to Sandy Roberton placing Matthews with Mooncrest, which was already re–releasing various of Roberton's B&C, Pegasus and Peg albums.

CREST 19   DECAMERON: Mammoth Special
1. Mammoth Special
2. Rock 'N' Roll Woman
3. Just Enough Like Home
4. A Glimpse Of Me
5. Late On Lady Day
6. Breakdown Of The Song

1. The Cheetah
2. Jan
3. Stonehouse
4. Parade
5. The Empty Space

Rel: Sep 1974[1]
RRP: £2.25[4]/
£2.41[1]

Cassette: ZCRES 19   Rel: Sep 1974[2]   RRP: £2.40[2]
8–track: Y8RES 19   Rel: Sep 1974[2]   RRP: £2.40[2]

Insert. Recorded for Vertigo but re–recorded and released on Mooncrest. Al Fenn explains: "... what was to be 'Mammoth Special' was first recorded for Vertigo, again produced by Sandy Roberton [who had produced the first LP for Vertigo] – Vertigo didn't like it, so we parted company and went to Mooncrest. There we recorded most of the tracks again – one or two fell by the wayside and were replaced by newer material, thereby losing the track on which our five fathers sang backing vocals."

The B&C Discography: 1968 to 1975

CREST 20   *NO RELEASE*

CREST 21   **CHILLI WILLI AND THE RED HOT PEPPERS: Bongos Over Balham**

1. Choo Choo Ch'Boogie
2. We Get Along
3. Desert Island Woman
4. All In A Dream
5. Fiddle Diddle

1. Breathe A Little
2. Truck Driving Girl
3. Jungle Song
4. Midnight Bus
5. Just Like The Devil
6. 9 – 5 Songwriting Man

Rel: Oct[4]/Nov '74[1]
RRP: £2.45[1]

Cassette: ZCRES 21   **Rel:** Oct 1974[2]   **RRP:** £2.40[2]
8-track: Y8RES 21   **Rel:** Oct 1974[2]   **RRP:** £2.40[2]

Inner sleeve. If there were a prize for the best sleeve on Mooncrest then this would win!

CREST 22   **STEELEYE SPAN: Hark The Village Wait**

1. A Calling–On Song
2. The Blacksmith
3. Fisherman's Wife
4. Blackleg Miner
5. Dark–Eyed Sailor
6. Copshawholme Fair

1. All Things Are Quite Silent
2. The Hills Of Glenmore
3. My Johnny Was A Shoemaker
4. Lowlands of Holland
5. Twa Corbies
6. One Night As I Lay On My Bed

Rel: Sep[4]/Nov '74[1]
RRP: £2.25[4]/
£2.45[1]

Cassette: ZCRES 22   **Rel:** Sep 1974[2]   **RRP:** £2.40[2]
8-track: Y8RES 22   **Rel:** Sep 1974[2]   **RRP:** £2.40[2]

The record was pressed by Lyntone with "LYN 13885" and "LYN 13886" scratched in the run–offs. Original 1970 RCA release (SF 8113) deleted the same month the Mooncrest version was issued [4].

CREST 23   **TIM HART AND MADDY PRIOR: Folk Songs Of Olde England Volume I**

1. Lish Young Buy-a-Broom
2. Adieu Sweet Lovely Nancy
3. Maid That's Deep In Love
4. The Rambling Sailor
5. Bruton Town
6. Farewell Nancy

1. The Daleman's Litany
2. The Brisk Young Butcher
3. The Stately Southerner
4. Who's The Fool Now
5. A Wager A Wager
6. Babes In The Wood
7. Adam And Eve

Rel: Nov 1974[1]
RRP: £2.45[1]

Cassette: ZCRES 23   **Rel:** Feb 1975[2]   **RRP:** £2.65[2]
8-track: Y8RES 23   **Rel:** Feb 1975[2]   **RRP:** £2.65[2]

Pressed by Lyntone with "LYN 13887" and "LYN 13888" scratched in run–offs (still there on the 1976 issue – probably old stock in new sleeves). The first Mooncrest sleeve was of a patchwork design, titled as above. Reissued by the resurrected Mooncrest label in 1976 with different sleeve design and the amended title "Folk Songs Of Old England–Volume I" ("Old" without the "e"). A much later Mooncrest reissue in yet another redesigned sleeve (with butterflies) reverted to "Olde".

Originally released in 1968 on Tepee (TPRM 104) and also released in 1969 on Tepee offshoot, Ad Rhythm (ARPS 3), in different sleeve design and side 1 and side 2 switched over for no readily explained reason. Both issues credited as "Folk Songs Of Old England" ("Old" without the "e") with the subtitle "Vol. 1" on the original Tepee release and "Volume 1" on the Ad Rhythm reissue. The original Tee Pee release seems to have been in mono only, whilst the Ad Rhythm reissue seems to have been stereo only. Ad Rhythm issue was deleted in 1974[4].

The B&C Discography: 1968 to 1975

CREST 24   ESRA MOHAWK: Essra Mohawk

1. New Skins For Old
2. Openin' My Love Doors
3. Full Fledged Woman
4. You're Finally Here
5. Summertime
6. Back In The Spirit

1. You Make Me Come To Pieces
2. I Cannot Forget
3. Song To An Unborn Soul
4. If I'm Gonna Go Crazy With Someone It Might As Well Be You
5. Magic Pen

Rel: Feb 1975[1]
RRP: £2.45[1]

Inner sleeve. No tape versions notified to *The New Cassettes & Cartridges* nor *Cassettes & Cartidges*.

CREST 25   MARTIN CARTHY: Shearwater
Rel: Feb 1975[4]   RRP: pres. £2.25
Refer to PEG 12 for track listing. Original Peg tape releases were still available.

CREST 26   TIM HART AND MADDY PRIOR: Folk Songs Of Olde England Volume II

1. My Son John
2. Earl John
3. Paddy Stole The Rope
4. The Gardener
5. The Bay Of Biscay
6. Queen Eleanor's Confession

1. Horn Of The Hunter
2. Copshawholme Fair
3. Oats And Beans
4. Fiddler's Green
5. Capt. Wedderburn's Courtship
6. Turkey Rhubarb
7. The Bold Fisherman

Rel: 1975
RRP: pres. £2.45

Cassette: ZCRES 26   Rel: May 1975[2]   RRP: £2.65[2]
8–track: Y8RES 26   Rel: May 1975[2]   RRP: £2.65[2]

Track 3, side 2 credited on sleeve as "Oats & Beans & Barley Grows" but as "Oats & Beans" on the label; track 5, side 2 credited on sleeve as "Captain" but as above on the label. The first Mooncrest sleeve was of a patchwork design, titled as above. Reissued by the resurrected Mooncrest label in 1976 with different sleeve design and the amended title "Folk Songs Of Old England–Volume II" ("Old" without the "e"). A much later Mooncrest reissue in yet another redesigned sleeve (with butterflies) reverted to "Olde".

Originally released in 1969 on Tepee (TPRM 105) and also released on Tepee offshoot, Ad Rhythm (ARPS 4) in different sleeve design. Both issues credited as "Folk Songs Of Old England" ("Old" without added "e") with the subtitle "Vol. 2" on the original Tepee release and "Volume 2" on the Ad Rhythm reissue. The original Tee Pee release seems to have been in mono only, whilst the Ad Rhythm reissue seems to have been stereo only. The Ad Rhythm issue deleted in 1974[4].

CREST 27   NAZARETH: Hair Of The Dog

1. Hair Of The Dog
2. Miss Misery
3. Guilty
4. Changin' Times

1. Beggars Day
2. Rose In The Heather
3. Whisky Drinkin' Woman
4. Please Don't Judas Me

Rel: Apr 1975[1]
RRP: £2.45[1]

Cassette: ZCRES 27   Rel: May 1975[2]   RRP: £2.65[2]
8–track: Y8RES 27   Rel: May 1975[2]   RRP: £2.65[2]
Inner sleeve.

CREST 28   DECAMERON: Beyond The Days (NOT RELEASED)
Rel: Jul 1975[1/4] (see below)   RRP: pres. £2.75[1] (see below)
Despite *Music Master* publications from 1976 on confidently stating a release date of July 1975 this was caught up in B&C's liquidation and issued instead by Transatlantic as *Third Light* in October 1975[4]. Al Fenn explains: "We recorded *Beyond the Days* with Tom Allom as producer for Mooncrest, with all artwork etc. done (dreadful!) but, unfortunately, B&C went down before its release. We then moved to Transatlantic, and it was released under the title of *Third Light*. The ... non existent ... version ... appears in *Record Collector* ... valued at £25!"

MOON sequence 7" singles

Most, but not all, releases were pressed up with the same track on both sides for promotional use. Where different (and known) this is noted. MOON 50 and 51, were notified to the trade for June 1975 release, but were caught up in B&C's liquidation and remained unreleased (unless anyone out there knows any different, that is). When Mooncrest was resurrected in 1976, these two numbers were reused for the first two new releases, which adds to the argument that the originally intended records were not issued.

MOON 1   **NAZARETH: Broken Down Angel / Witchdoctor**
Rel: 23 Mar 1973[8]
Promotional copies with the same track on both sides came in a yellow, printed die–cut single sleeve with details of the first two 7" releases on the label.

MOON 2   **LIBIDO: Hold On To Your Fire / Weren't Born A Man**
Rel: 23 Mar 1973[8]
Promotional copies have the same track on both sides and these, presumably, came in promotional sleeves as per MOON 1.

MOON 3   **LIGHTHOUSE: Sunny Days / Lonely Places**
Rel: 20 Apr 1973[3]

MOON 4   **A. AND A. NORTH: My Star / I Love You Because**
Rel: 20 Apr 1973[3]

MOON 5   **HOTSHOTS: Snoopy Versus The Red Baron / What Do You Say**
Rel: 4 May 1973[3]

MOON 6   **ROCKMORE WILLIAMS: It Was Her / I'm A Man**
Rel: 11 May 1973[8]/11 Jan 1974[3]

MOON 7   **OCTOPUS: Hey Na Na / Future Feelings**
Rel: 16 Jun[3]/Jul 1973[5]

MOON 8   **DONNA MARIE NEWMAN: Born Too Late / Everybody's Saying Goodbye**
Rel: 15 Jun 1973[3]

MOON 9   **NAZARETH: Bad Bad Boy / Hard Living / Spinning Top**
Rel: 6 Jul 1973[3]
Picture sleeve.

MOON 10   **WOOLLY: Sunshine Souvenirs / Living And Loving You**
Rel: 27 Jul 1973[3/8]

MOON 11   **STEVE FELDMAN: Waitin' For The Day To Come / Crystal Dawn**
Rel: 10 Aug 1973[3]

MOON 12   **HOTSHOTS: Battle Of New Orleans / Knockin' On The Door**
Rel: 14 Sep 1973[3]

MOON 13   **DANDY LIVINGSTONE: Black Star / All Strung Out On You**
Rel: 14 Sep[3]/30 Nov 1973[3]
Labels are modified to include Livingstone's face.

MOON 14   NAZARETH: This Flight Tonight / Called Her Name
Rel: 21 Sep 1973[3]

MOON 15   ROCKMORE WILLIAMS: Lady Rock / Junkyard Blues
Rel: 19 Oct 1973[3]

MOON 16   DONNA MARIE NEWMAN: Daddy / Sing Me Songs
Rel: 26 Oct 1973[3]

MOON 17   STU NUNNERY: Sally From Syracuse / Madelaine
Rel: 2 Nov 1973[3/8]

MOON 18   CINDY MILLER AND THE FRANCIS COOMBE SCHOOL CHOIR: Dubious Circus Company / Baby, I Need You Now
Rel: 9 Nov 1973[3]

MOON 19   SPIKE O'BRIEN'S CIRCUS: Poor Little Fred / Soggy Moggy Bogged Down Blues
Rel: 16 Nov 1973[3]

MOON 20   HOTSHOTS: Yesterday Man / Jerusalem Rock
Rel: 23 Nov 1973[3]
Copies exist with the b-side label on both sides.

MOON 21   WOODY: Saturday Woman / Zoo Baby
Rel: 14 Dec 1973[3]
The New Singles miscredits the artist as "Smiley" for reasons unknown.

MOON 22   NAZARETH: Shanghai'd In Shanghai / Love, Now You're Gone
Rel: 1 Mar 1974[3]

MOON 23   STU NUNNERY: Madelaine / Sally From Syracuse
Rel: 11 Apr 1974[3]
Basically a reissue of MOON 17 with the sides reversed.

MOON 24   GORDON JACKSON: On The Road To Munich / The Boardroom Reel
Rel: 26 Apr 1974[3/8]
Jim Parker and Hugh Murphy took time out from working on Charisma's John Betjeman albums to do something similar for *Upstairs, Downstairs* actor, Jackson.

MOON 25   ARNOLD CORNS: Hang On To Yourself / Man In The Middle
Rel: 17 May 1974 [3/8] (del: 1976[5])
Reissue of the B&C single, CB 189.

MOON 26   TIM MOORE: When You Close Your Eyes / Aviation Man
Rel: May[5]/31 Jun 1974[3]

MOON 27   IAN MATTHEWS: Met Her On A Plane / Knowing The Game
Rel: 7 Jun 1974[3]

MOON 28   JONNY SUMMA: Seventeen / Young Girl
Rel: 7 Jun 1974[3]

MOON 29   ALBATROSS: Rock 'N' Roll Boogie Man / Witchi Witchi Lady
Rel: 5 Jul 1974[3]

MOON 30   HOTSHOTS: Caribbean / Together
Rel: 19 Jul 1974[3]

MOON 31   ROCKMORE WILLIAMS: Roll Me Over Again / Junkyard Blues
Rel: 26 Jul 1974[3]
Junkyard Blues was previously issued as the b–side of MOON 15.

MOON 32   TIM MOORE: Charmer / Second Avenue
Rel: Sep[7]/4 Oct 1974[3]

MOON 33   JOHNNIE RICCO: Run Around Sue / Scamp Stamp
Rel: 4 Oct 1974[3]

MOON 34   DECAMERON: Rock And Roll Away / Twinset And Pearls
Rel: 25 Oct 1974[3]

MOON 35   THE ANGELETTES: I Surrender / Goodbye Jon
Rel: 1 Nov 1974[3]

MOON 36   ALBATROSS: Anything I Want To / Bournemouth Rock
Rel: 8 Nov 1974[3]

MOON 37   NAZARETH: Love Hurts / Down
Rel: 8 Nov 1974[3]

MOON 38   NO RELEASE

MOON 39   SCOTT ENGLISH: Brandy / Lead Me Back
Rel: 31 Jan[3]/Feb 1975[7]

MOON 40   CHILLI WILLI AND THE RED HOT PEPPERS: Breathe A Little / Friday Song
Rel: 7 Feb 1975[3] (del: 1977[5])

MOON 41   TIM MOORE: A Fool Like You / Aviation Man
Rel: 21 Feb 1975[3]
Aviation Man was previously issued as the b–side of MOON 26. Promotional copies have the normal track listing.

MOON 42   ALBATROSS: Darlin' / The Band Played On
Rel: 28 Feb 1975[3] (del: 1978[5])

MOON 43   PLAYGROUNDS: This Old Man / Always Friends
Rel: 21 Mar 1975[3]
Promotional copies have normal track listing but with a large "A" printed on the a–side.

MOON 44   NAZARETH: Hair Of The Dog / Too Bad, Too Sad
Rel: 14 Mar 1975[3]

The B&C Discography: 1968 to 1975

MOON 45   **DECAMERON: Breakdown Of The Song / Twinset And Pearls**
Rel: 11 Apr 1975[3] (del: 1977[5])
Twinset and Pearls previously issued as the b–side of MOON 34. Promotional copies have normal track listing.

MOON 46   **ARLAN GREEN: Rock Hotel / Rock Hotel (PROMOS ONLY?)**
Rel: not advised to *The New Singles*
The only copies to come to light are promotional pressings with *Rock Hotel* on both sides. It is possible that there are proper copies out there but, if so, where?

MOON 47   **NAZARETH: My White Bicycle / Miss Misery**
Rel: 25 Apr 1975[3]

MOON 48   **NO RELEASE**

MOON 49   **GARY BENSON: Don't Throw It All Away / This House**
Rel: 6 Jun 1975[3]

MOON 50   **MAGNIFICENT MERCURY BROTHERS: New Girl In School / What About Us / Why Do Fools Fall In Love / (I'm Not A) Juvenile Delinquent (NOT RELEASED)**
Rel: 27 Jun 1975[3] (see below)
Scheduled for release as above though caught up in B&C's liquidation and not issued. The Magnificent Mercury Brothers were really Decameron. Al Fenn explains: "... the Magnificent Mercury Brothers songs were destined for an EP on Mooncrest – the whole thing came from the fact that we would slip a Beach Boys/doo wop song into our normal set (light relief from some of the rest of our songs). These would go down a storm with folk club audiences ... [Mooncrest label manager] Jim Flynn saw this reaction more than once, and said we had to record them. They were recorded at the same time as *Beyond the Days* ... but never got to the artwork stage ... Transatlantic took them on, and cautiously released *New Girl In School* which got onto the Radio One playlist ..." Transatlantic released the four tracks as two singles, *New Girl In School* / *What About Us* (BIG 532) and *Why Do Fools Fall In Love* / *(I'm Not A) Juvenile Delinquent* (BIG 536). *New Girl In School* got a reissue on Transatlantic's new Logo imprint in 1978 (GO 107).

MOON 51   **THE FORTUNES: These Are The Good Old Days / Holy Roller (NOT RELEASED)**
Rel: 20 Jun 1975[3] (del: 1977[5]) (see below)
Although notified as a June 1975 release to trade publications, it is more than likely that this was caught up in the B&C liquidation and that the first distribution (if indeed any were pressed) was by the resurrected Trojan. The single is listed as unreleased on the Fortunes' official fan website (http://www.songwriters.4t.com/) and this would seem to be accurate in that no copies are known to have cropped up on the collectors' circuit (other than rumour of a one–sided Trident acetate, that is). If this latter is true then the notified deletion date seems a little mysterious. Perhaps 1977 represents the date at which Trojan got fed up with being asked for copies.

People

Various releases, including cassette and 8–track versions, were listed as on catalogue as late as 1979. As from 1976, these were listed as distributed by the resurrected Trojan, and probably represented unsold original stock. The only record confirmed as repressed post–liquidation was Donna Summer's *The Hostage* (PEO 115), this following her recent success on the GTO label (PEO 118 may also have been repressed).

PLEO sequence LPs

PLEO 1 REUBEN WILSON: The Cisco Kid
1. The Cisco Kid
2. The Last Tango In Paris
3. Superfly
4. We've Only Just Begun

1. Snaps
2. Groove Grease
3. The Look Of Love

Rel: Nov 1973[1]
RRP: £1.99[1]/
£2.14[4]
Del: 1975[5]

Cassette: ZCPLE 1   Rel: May 1974[2] (del 1977[5])   RRP: £2.45[2]
8–track: Y8PLE   Rel: May 1974[2] (del 1977[5])   RRP: £2.45[2]

PLEO 2 LARRY WILLIS: Inner Crisis
1. Out On The Cost
2. 153rd Street Theme
3. Inner Crisis

1. Bahamian Street Dance
2. For A Friend
3. Journey's End

Rel: Nov 1973[1]
RRP: £1.99[1]/
£2.14[4]
Del: 1975[5]

Cassette: ZCPLE 2   Rel: May 1974[2]   RRP: £2.45[2]
8–track: Y8PLE 2   Rel: May 1974[2] (del 1977[5])   RRP: £2.45[2]

PLEO 3 O'DONEL LEVY: Dawn Of A New Day
1. Dawn Of A New Day
2. Baa Waa
3. I Wanna Be Where You Are
4. Where Is The Love
5. People Make The World Go Round

1. Maiden Voyage
2. Super Woman
3. I Want To Make It With You
4. Goin' On To Detroit

Rel: Nov 1973[1]
RRP: £1.99[1]/
£2.14[4]
Del: 1975[5]

Cassette: ZCPLE 3   Rel: May 1974[2]   RRP: £2.45[2]
8–track: Y8PLE 3   Rel: May 1974[2] (del 1977[5])   RRP: £2.45[2]

PLEO 4 JUNIOR PARKER: You Don't Have To Be Black To Love The Blues
1. Five Years Long
2. Tin Pan Alley
3. Blue Shadows Falling
4. That's Alright
5. Way Back Home

1. I Need Love So Bad
2. Look On Yonders Wall
3. Man Or Mouse
4. Sweet Home Chicago
5. I Like Your Smile

Rel: Nov 1973[1]
RRP: £1.99[1]/
£2.14[4]
Del: 1975[5]

Cassette: ZCPLE 4   Rel: May 1974[2]   RRP: £2.45[2]
8–track: Y8PLE 4   Rel: May 1974[2]   RRP: £2.45[2]

PLEO 5 RAMON MORRIS: Sweet Sister Funk
1. First Come, First Serve
2. Wijinia
3. Sweet Sister Funk

1. Sweat
2. Don't Ask Me
3. Lord Sideways
4. People Make The World Go Round

Rel: Nov 1973[1]
RRP: £1.99[1]/
£2.14[4]
Del: 1975[5]

Cassette: ZCPLE 5   Rel: May 1974[2]   RRP: £2.45[2]
8–track: Y8PLE 5   Rel: May 1974[2] (del 1977[5])   RRP: £2.45[2]

The B&C Discography: 1968 to 1975

PLEO 6   **CARMEN McRAE: It Takes A Whole Lot Of Human Feeling**

1. It Takes A Whole Lot of Human Feeling
2. I Fall In Love Too Easily
3. Hey John
4. Where Are The Words
5. Nice Work If You Can Get It

1. Straighten Up And Fly Right
2. Inside A Silent Tear
3. Imagination
4. The Right To Love
5. All The Things You Are

Rel: Nov 1973[1]
RRP: £1.99[1]/£2.14[5]

Cassette: ZCPLE 6   **Rel:** May 1974[2] (del 1977[5])   **RRP:** £2.45[2]
8–track: Y8PLE 6   **Rel:** May 1974[2] (del 1977[5])   **RRP:** £2.45[2]

PLEO 7   **DELLA REESE: Let Me In Your Life**

1. Let Me In Your Life
2. Lay Baby Lay
3. If Loving You Is Wrong (I Don't Want To Be Right)
4. Being Green
5. Let's Start All Over Again

1. Fire And Rain/Bye Bye Love
2. Never Can Say Good–Bye/Let's Stay Together
3. Funny
4. Who Is She And What Is She To You

Rel: Nov 1973[1]
RRP: £1.99[1]/£2.14[4]
Del: 1975[5]

Cassette: ZCPLE 7   **Rel:** May 1974[2]   **RRP:** £2.45[2]
8–track: Y8PLE 7   **Rel:** May 1974[2]   **RRP:** £2.45[2]

PLEO 8   **NO RELEASE**

PLEO 9   **CHICK COREA: Sundance**

1. The Brain
2. Song Of Wind

1. Converge
2. Sundance

Rel: Feb 1974[4]
RRP: £2.25[4]

Cassette: ZCPLE 9   **Rel:** Jun 1974[2] (del 1977[5])   **RRP:** £2.45[2]
8–track: Y8PLE 9   **Rel:** Jun 1974[2]   **RRP:** £2.45[2]

PLEO 10   **GROOVE HOLMES: American Pie**

1. American Pie
2. St. Thomas
3. Catherine
4. Fingers

1. It's Impossible
2. Rainy Day
3. Who Can I Turn To

Rel: Feb 1974[4]
RRP: £2.25[4]

Cassette: ZCPLE 10   **Rel:** Jul 1974[2]   **RRP:** £2.45[2]
8–track: Y8PLE 10   **Rel:** Jul 1974[2]   **RRP:** £2.45[2]

PLEO 11   **DAKOTA STATON: Madame Foo–Foo**

1. Let It Be Me
2. Congratulations To Someone
3. Let Me Off Uptown
4. A House Is Not A Home
5. Blues For Tasty

1. A Losing Battle
2. Deep In A Dream
3. Confessin' The Blues
4. Candy
5. Moonglow

Rel: Feb[4]/Mar '74[1]
RRP: £2.25[1]

Cassette: ZCPLE 11   **Rel:** Jun 1974[2]   **RRP:** £2.45[2]
8–track: Y8PLE 11   **Rel:** Jun 1974[2] (del 1977[5])   **RRP:** £2.45[2]

PLEO 12   **DORIS TROY: Stretchin' Out**

1. Stretchin' Out
2. All I Have Is Written In Your Eyes
3. Don't Let Me Be Lonely Tonight
4. Jesus Is All The World To Me
5. Reconsider Our Love
6. In My Father's Home

1. Black Star
2. Way Back Home
3. Don't Tell Your Mama
4. Tell Me
5. Listen To The Music

Rel: Mar 1974[1]
RRP: £2.25[1]
Del: 1975[5]

The B&C Discography: 1968 to 1975

Cassette: ZCPLE 12	**Rel:** Jun 1974[2]	**RRP:** £2.45[2]
8–track: Y8PLE 12	**Rel:** Jun 1974[2] (del 1977[5])	**RRP:** £2.45[2]

PLEO 13 — BABY WASHINGTON AND DON GARDNER: Lay A Little Lovin' On Me

1. Lay A Little Lovin' On Me
2. Forever
3. I've Got To Break Away (Washington)
4. Just Stand By Me (Gardner)
5. Baby Let Me Get Close To You

1. I Just Want To Be Near To You
2. Is It True I Fell In Love Again
3. Carefree (Washington)
4. We're Gonna Make It Big (Gardner)
5. Can't Get Over Losing You (Washington)

Rel: Mar 1974[1]
RRP: £2.25[1]
Del: 1975[5]

Cassette: ZCPLE 13   **Rel:** Jul 1974[10]   **RRP:** prob. £2.45
8–track: Y8PLE 13   **Rel:** Jul 1974[10] (del 1977[5])   **RRP:** prob. £2.45

Some tracks are solo, as indicated above, whilst the rest are joint recordings.

PLEO 14 — JIMMY McGRIFF: Fly Dude

1. Everyday I Have The Blues
2. Jumping The Blues
3. Healin' Feeling
4. Cotton Boy Blues

1. Yardbird Suite
2. The Groove Fly
3. It's You I Adore
4. Butterfly

Rel: Apr[4]/May '74[1]
RRP: £2.25[1]

Cassette: ZCPLE 14   **Rel:** Jul 1974[2]   **RRP:** £2.45[2]
8–track: Y8PLE 14   **Rel:** Jul 1974[2] (del 1977[5])   **RRP:** £2.45[2]

PLEO 15 — JOE THOMAS: Joy Of Cookin'

1. Joyful, Joyful
2. Down Home
3. Chile Con Carmen

1. Thank You (Fall Etin Me Be Mice Elf Agin)
2. Soul Sermon
3. Mike
4. Dr. Ritota

Rel: Feb[4]/May[1]/Jun 1974[1]
RRP: £2.25[1]

Cassette: ZCPLE 15   **Rel:** Jul 1974[2]   **RRP:** £2.45[2]
8–track: Y8PLE 15   **Rel:** Jul 1974[2] (del 1977[5])   **RRP:** £2.45[2]

PLEO 16 — JIMMY McGRIFF AND GROOVE HOLMES: Giants Of The Organ Come Together

1. Licks A' Plenty
2. Out Of Nowhere
3. The Squirrel

1. Finger Lickin' Good
2. How High The Moon
3. Things Ain't What They Used To Be

Rel: Apr[4]/May '74[1]
RRP: £2.25[1]

Cassette: ZCPLE 16   **Rel:** Jun 1974[2]   **RRP:** £2.45[2]
8–track: Y8PLE 16   **Rel:** Jun 1974[2] (del 1977[5])   **RRP:** £2.45[2]

8–track deleted 1977 if you look under McGriff, but still on catalogue if you look under Holmes!

PLEO 17 — JIMMY McGRIFF: Friday The 13th. Cook County Jail.

1. Freedom Suite, Part I
2. Freedom Suite, Part II

1. Green Dolphin Street
2. Everything Happens To Me
3. Cherokee

Rel: unconfirmed
RRP: prob. £2.25

Cassette: ZCPLE 17   **Rel:** Jul 1974[2]   **RRP:** £2.45[2]
8–track: Y8PLE 17   **Rel:** Jul 1974[2] (del 1977[5])   **RRP:** £2.45[2]

The B&C Discography: 1968 to 1975

PLEO 18   JUNIOR PARKER: Love Ain't Nothin' But A Business Going On

1. Love Ain't Nothin' But A Business Goin' On
2. The Outside Man
3. Darling Depend On Me
4. Taxman
5. Rivers Invitation

1. I Wonder Where Our Love Has Gone
2. Just To Hold My Hand
3. You Know I Love You
4. Lady Madonna
5. Tomorrow Never Knows

Rel: between Apr and Jun '74[12]
RRP: £2.25[4]
Del: 1975[5]

Cassette: ZCPLE 18   Rel: Jul 1974[2]   RRP: £2.45[2]
8–track: Y8PLE 18   Rel: Jul 1974[2]   RRP: £2.45[2]

PLEO 19   JIMMY McGRIFF: Let's Stay Together

1. Let's Stay Together
2. Tiki
3. The Theme From Shaft
4. What's Going On

1 Old Grad Dad
2. Georgia On My Mind
3. April In Paris

Rel: unconfirmed
RRP: £2.25[4]

Cassette: ZCPLE 19   Rel: Sep 1974[2]   RRP: £2.40[2]
8–track: Y8PLE 19   Rel: Sep 1974[2] (del 1977[5])   RRP: £2.40[2]

PLEO 20   RUEBEN WILSON: The Sweet Life

1. Inner City Blues
2. Creampuff
3. Sugar

1. I'll Take You There
2. The Sweet Life
3. Never Can Say Goodbye

Rel: Jun 1974[4]
RRP: £2.25[4]
Del: 1975[5]

Cassette: ZCPLE 20   Rel: Sep 1974[2] (del 1977[5])   RRP: £2.45[2]
8–track: Y8PLE 20   Rel: Sep 1974[2] (del 1977[5])   RRP: £2.45[2]

PLEO 21   O'DONEL LEVY: Breeding Of Mind

1. We've Only Just Begun
2. It's Too Late
3. Breeding Of Mind
4. Cherries
5. On Broadway

1. Ideal
2. Never Can Say Goodbye
3. Let's Stay Together
4. The Chocolate Horse
5. Angel Eyes

Rel: Jun 1974[4]
RRP: £2.25[4]
Del: 1975[5]

Cassette: ZCPLE 21   Rel: Sep 1974[2]   RRP: £2.40[2]
8–track: Y8PLE 21   Rel: Sep 1974[2] (del 1977[5])   RRP: £2.40[2]

PLEO 22   GEORGE FREEMAN: New Improved Funk

1. New Improved Funk
2. Daffy
3. Happy Fingers
4. All In The Game
5. Big Finish

1. Guitar Lover Man
2. Good Morning Heartache
3. Some Enchanted Evening
4. Confirmed Truth

Rel: Jun 1974[4]
RRP: £2.25[4]

Cassette: ZCPLE 22   Rel: Sep 1974[2]   RRP: £2.40[2]
8–track: Y8PLE 22   Rel: Sep 1974[2] (del: 1977[5])   RRP: £2.40[2]

PLEO 23   JIMMY McGRIFF: If You're Ready Come Go With Me

1. If You're Ready Come Go With Me
2. Shuckin' And Jivin'
3. Dig On It
4. Bug Out
5. Fat Cakes
6. Super Funk

1. Let's Stay Together
2. The Bird
3. Plain Brown Bag
4. Jumpin' The Blues
5. Tiki
6. Ain't It Funky Now

Rel: Jun 1974[4]
RRP: £2.25[4]

No tape versions notified to T*he New Cassettes & Cartridges* nor *Cassettes & Cartridges*.

PLEO 24   VARIOUS ARTISTS: Super Sweet Soul

1. Get On Board (Wee Three)
2. Rockspring Rail Road Station
   (Tom Green)
3. Black Foxy Woman
   (Chuck Armstrong)
4. Care Free (Baby Washington)
5. Check Your Bucket (Eddie Bo)
6. Super Sweet Girl Of Mine
   (Five Miles Out)
7. We're Gonna Make It Big
   (Don Gardner)
8. My Sweet Baby (The Esquires)

1. Get It While You Can
   (Wilbert Harrison)
2. Dynamite Explodes
   (Gentle Persuasion)
3. Get Some (Wee Willie And
   The Winners)
4. It Ain't Easy (Brother James And
   Sugar Mama)
5. Set Your Mind Free (Five Miles Out)
6. Just Keep On Truckin'
   (Backyard Heavies)
7. Soul Makossa (The Gaytones)
8. Funky Buttercup (The Chosen Few)

Rel: Jul[4]/Aug '74[1]
RRP: £2.25[4]/
£2.45[1]

Cassette: ZCPLE 24
8–track: Y8PLE 24

Rel: Sep 1974[2]
Rel: Sep 1974[2] (del 1977[5])

RRP: £2.45[2]
RRP: £2.45[2]

PLEO 25   THE BROTHERS: Disco–Soul

1. Get Dancin'
2. Never Can Say Goodbye
3. Thanks A Million
4. In the Pocket
5. Kung Fu Fighting

1. You're The First, The Last, My
   Everything
2. Fire
3. Everybody Loves A Winner
4. Are You Ready For This
5. Doctor's Orders

Rel: Apr 1975[1/4]
RRP: £2.45[1]

No tape versions notified to *The New Cassettes & Cartridges* not *Cassettes & Cartridges*.

PLED sequence double LP

PLED 501   JIMMY McGRIFF: Black And Blues

Record 1, side 1
1. Blue Groove Part 1
2. Blues For A Broken Down Funky
   Old Bus
3. Mocha

Record 2, side 1
1. Bahama
2. Amen
3. Hey, Mrs Jones

Record 1, side 2
1. Harp–er
2. Lonesome Road
3. Mack The Knife

Record 2, side 2
1. Blue Groove Part 2
2. Penthouse Serenade
3. Pennies From Heaven

Rel: Nov 1973[1]/
Mar 1974[1]
RRP: £3.49[1]

Cassette: ZCPLD 501
8–track: Y8PLD 501

Rel: May 1974[1]
Rel: May 1974[1] (del 1977[5])

RRP: £3.20[1]
RRP: £3.20[1]

PLE sequence tape–only release

ZCPLE 101/Y8PLE 101   VARIOUS ARTISTS: Listen To The People

1. Listen To The Music (Doris Troy)
2. Tomorrow Never Knows (Junior Parker)
3. Things Ain't What They Used To Be* (Jimmy McGriff And Groove Holmes)
4. I'll Take You There (Reubin Wilson)
5. Sundance* (Chick Corea)
6. Thank You (Joe Thomas)
7. Dynamite Explodes (Gentle Persuasion)
8. Forever (Baby Washington And Don Gardner)
9. Cherokee (Lucky Thompson)
10. Where Is The Love (O'Donel Levy)
11. Out On The Coast (Larry Willis)
12. Let's Start Over All Again (Della Reese)

1. People Make The World Go Round (Ramon Morris)
2. We're Gonna Make It Big (Don Gardner)
3. I Need Your Love So Bad (Junior Parker)
4. American Pie (Groove Holmes)
5. A House Is Not A Home (Dakota Staton)
6. Never Can Say Goodbye (Reuben Wilson)
7. Lonely Days Lonely Nights (Don Downing)
8. Get On Board (Wee Three)
9. Straighten Up And Fly Right (Carmen McRae)
10. New Improved Funk (George Freeman)
11. Breeding Of Mind (O'Donel Levy)
12. Just Can't Get You Out Of My Mind (Baby Washington)
13. Amen (Jimmy McGriff)

Cassette: ZCPEO 101 **Rel:** Jul 1974[2] **RRP:** £2.45[2]
8–track: Y8PEO 101 **Rel:** Jul 1974[2] (del 1977[5]) **RRP:** £2.45[2]

Track listing from the cassette version. The two tracks marked * are edited versions.

PEO sequence 7"singles

As per B&C policy many releases were pressed up with the same track on both sides for promotional use. Where different (and known) this is noted. Some singles were issued in a company sleeve advertising *Black Music* magazine on one side with adverts for People, Ashanti, Dragon and Trojan product on the other.

PEO 101   BABY WASHINGTON AND DON GARDNER: Forever / Baby Let Me Get Close To You
Rel: 20 Jul[8]/27 Jul 1973[3]/Mar 1974[5]
Promotional copies have same track listing as stock copies. *Music Master* (5th ed.) lists release date as both July 1973 and March 1974.

PEO 102   DON DOWNING: Lonely Days, Lonely Nights / I'm So Proud Of You
Rel: 24 Aug 1973[3]

PEO 103   GENTLE PERSUASION: Dynamite Explodes / Bring It On Home
Rel: 19 Oct 1973[3/8]

PEO 104   WEE THREE: Get On Board / Get On Board (Instrumental)
Rel: 26 Oct 1973[3/8]

PEO 105   BABY WASHINGTON: Just Can't Get You Out of My Mind / You (Just A Dream)
Rel: 2 Nov 1973[3]
Promotional copies have same track listing as stock copies.

The B&C Discography: 1968 to 1975

PEO 106   **DELLA REECE:** *Who Is She And What Is She To You / If Loving You Is Wrong (I Don't Want To Be Right)*
Rel: 11 Jan[3]/1 Mar 1974[3]

PEO 107   **BABY WASHINGTON:** *I've Got To Break Away / Can't Get Over Losing You*
Rel: 15 Feb 1974[3]

PEO 108   **DON DOWNING:** *Dream World / The Miracle*
Rel: 8 Mar 1974[3] (del: 1976[5])

PEO 109   **RUEBEN WILSON:** *I'll Take You There / The Cisco Kid*
Rel: 29 Mar 1974[3]

PEO 110   **KRISSI K:** *Stick Up / Who Do You Think You Are*
Rel: 10 May 1974[3]

PEO 111   **WESTSIDE:** *Running In And Out Of My Life / Highway Demon*
Rel: 17 May 1974[3]

PEO 112   **DORIS TROY:** *Stretchin' Out / Don't Tell Your Mama*
Rel: 31 May 1974[3]

PEO 113   **J. KELLY AND THE PREMIERS:** *She Calls Me Baby / Signed, Sealed And Delivered*
Rel: not notified to *The New Singles*

PEO 114   **BARRY SMITH:** *Hold On To It / Hold On to It (Version)*
Rel: not notified to *The New Singles*

PEO 115   **DONNA SUMMER:** *The Hostage / Let's Work Together Now*
Rel: 4 Oct 1974[3]
Original copies have four prong die–cut centres. Later, solid–centre copies exist with updated label credits – these were issued by the resuscitated Trojan during September 1976[5] to capitalise on Summer's two 1976 chart successes on the GTO label.

PEO 116   **WEE WILLIE AND THE WINNERS:** *I Don't Know What You Got But I Know What You Need (Vocal) / I Don't Know What You Got But I Know What You Need (Instrumental?)*
Rel: 8 Nov[3]/11 Nov 1974[8]
Various recent sources list "(Part 1)" and "(Part 2)" after the titles. However, the a–side suffix as above is confirmed (on demo copies at least). The b–side suffix is not confirmed. US copies on Shotgun include "Part I" and "Part II".

PEO 117   **JIMMY JAMES AND THE VAGABONDS:** *Help Yourself / Why*
Rel: not notified to *The New Singles*
This was later issued on Trojan as TOP 1 in May 1975[3/5] and again on the resurrected Trojan label's Miami sub label as MIA 404 in September 1976[5].

PEO 118   **THE BROTHERS:** *In The Pocket / Everybody Loves A Winner*
Rel: 18 Apr 1975[3] (del: 1977[5])
Some copies include a Trojan logo on the labels. These have differences in sizing and placing of various credits and include a 1975 publication date, whilst the normal version says 1974. The guess is that this was repressed by the resurrected Trojan label.

PEO 119   *BARRY SMITH: Hold On To It / Hold On To It (Version)*
Rel: 13 Jun 1975[3]/Jul 1975[5]
This seems to be a straight reissue of PEO 114.

Promotional 7" EP

The BCP sequence was used over several B&C–related labels. Most so far identified were for B&C, Charisma or Pegasus/Peg artists. Only one record has been discovered with People label material, and that only on one side with the other dedicated to Action label material. All tracks are excerpts.

BCP 16   *VARIOUS ARTISTS: untitled*

1. Forever (Don Gardner And Baby Washington)
2. Lonely Days, Lonely Nights (Don Downing)

1. Check Your Bucket (Eddie Bo)
2. Get It While You Can (Wilbert Harrison)

Label: see below

A–side label is the People label design, whilst the b–side is the Action label design (AC3).

Dragon

Island set up Dragon in early 1973 to showcase Byron Lee's productions. In August 1973 Mooncrest acquired the license for marketing, distribution and promotion. All LPs were redistributed by Mooncrest with updated sleeve and label credits except for *The Dynamic Sounds Of Jamaica Vol 1* (HELP 9), which remained on catalogue as an Island release as late as 1979. Other Dragon label records were also listed as on catalogue as late as 1979, these now distributed by Trojan (most probably represented unsold original stock).

DRLS sequence LPs

Island–era releases

DRLS 5001   BYRON LEE AND THE DRAGONAIRES: Reggay Roun' The World

1. Breakfest In Bed
2. Cotton Jenny
3. Three Bells
4. Howdy Tenky
5. Popcorn
6. Smoke Gets In Your Eyes

1. Black On
2. City Of New Orleans
3. In The Mood
4. Your Love Is Amazing
5. Back Stabbers
6. Spanish Lace

Rel: 1973
RRP: £2.14[4]

Cassette: ZCDRL 5001   **Rel:** Sep 1974[2]   **RRP:** £2.40[2]
8–track: Y8DRL 5001   **Rel:** Sep 1974[2] (del 1977[5])   **RRP:** £2.40[2]

Title above as credited on labels: sleeve credits "Reggae Around The World". Original release via Island. Later copies confirmed with "Marketed by B&C Records" text on labels and sleeve.

DRLS 5002   TOOTS AND THE MAYTELS: Funky Kingston

1. Sit Right Down
2. Pomps And Pride
3. Louie Louie
4. I Can't Believe

1. Redemption Song
2. Daddy
3. Funky Kingston
4. It Was Written Down

Rel: 1973
RRP: £2.14[4]

Track 2, side 1 as credited on label: sleeve credits "Pomp and Pride". Later copies replaced Island credits with "Marketed by B&C Records". Following B&C's liquidation, Island reissued this as ILPS 9186 in April 1976[5] but the resurrected B&C/Trojan also reissued it on the original catalogue number in June 1976. It is possible that this latter reissue was really a redistribution of unsold B&C–era stock. No tape versions notified to *The New Cassettes & Cartridges* nor *Cassettes & Cartridges* though probably released at some point either by Island or Mooncrest, which a 1977 deletion date[5] suggests.

Mooncrest–era releases

DRLS 5003   VARIOUS ARTISTS: 20 Dragon Hits

1. I'm So Fed Up (Rocking Horse)
2. Happy Homecoming (Fabulous Flames)
3. What A Festival (Eric Donaldson)
4. Say Wonderful Things (Ken Parker)
5. Festival Tide (Marvin Brooks)
6. Rasta No Born (Jackie Brown)
7. Watergate Affair (Tommy McCook)
8. Our Rendezvous (Freddie McKay)
9. Stages In Life (Dennis Brown)
10. Dr. Who (I. Roy)

1. Conqueror (Stranger And Gladdy)
2. Version Festival (I. Roy And Eric)
3. I Wonder (Jimmy London)
4. The Great Tommy McCook (Tommy McCook)
5. Hot Cross Bun (Big Youth)
6. Happiness (Kitty)
7. Love I Festival (Adina Edwards)
8. Feel No Pain (Jackie Brown)
9. Jennie (Jimmy London)
10. Simpleton (The Cordells)

Rel: Nov 1973
RRP: £2.19[1]
   £2.14[4]
Del: 1976[5]

Listed in *The New Records* under Island even though issued via Mooncrest. No tape versions notified to *The New Cassettes & Cartridges* nor *Cassettes & Cartridges*.

DRLS 5004 TOOTS AND THE MAYTELS: In the Dark
1. Got To Be There
2. In The Dark
3. Having A Party
4. Time Tough
5. I See You
6. Take a Look In The Mirror

1. Take Me Home Country Roads
2. Fever
3. Love Gonna Walk Out On Me
4. Revolution
5. 54–36
6. Sailing On

Rel: Sep 1974[4]
RRP: £2.25[4]
Del: 1975[5]

Cassette: ZCDRL 5004
8–track: Y8DRL 5004

Rel: Sep 1974[2]
Rel: Sep 1974[2] (del: 1977[5])

RRP: £2.40[2]
RRP: £2.40[2]

DRLS 5005 FREDDIE McKAY: Lonely Man
1. Lonely Man
2. I'm Not Your Love
3. Where Can I Find True Love
4. I'm A Free Man
5. Peace In The Garden

1. If You Should Dream My Life Over
2. Losing Your Love
3. Black Beauty
4. If You Must Go
5. 100 lbs Of Clay

Rel: Feb[1/4]/
Mar 1975[1]
RRP: £2.25[1]

No tape versions notified to *The New Cassettes & Cartridges* nor *Cassettes & Cartridges*.

DRLS 5006 BYRON LEE AND THE DRAGONAIRES: The Midas Touch
1. Up Park Camp
2. None Shall Escape The Judgement
3. Girl We Got A Date
4. You Can't Blame The Youth
5. Here I Am (Come And Take Me)

1. I Shot The Sheriff
2. You Must Believe
3. My Girl
4. Road Block
5. Ode To Billy Joe

Rel: Mar[1]/
Apr '75[1/4]
RRP: £2.25

Cassette: ZCDRL 5006
8–track: Y8DRL 5006

Rel: May 1975[2]
Rel: May 1975[2] (del 1977[5])

RRP: £2.56[2]
RRP: £2.65[2]

DRLS 5007 NO RELEASE

DRLS 5008 HOPETOWN LEWIS: Dynamic Hopetown Lewis
1. Drift Away
2. Pied Piper
3. Keep On Singing
4. Working It Down To The Bone
5. Pick Yourself Up
6. God's Little Children

1. Show Me Some Loving
2. Goodbye Yesterday
3. Leaving Babylon
4. Take My Heart
5. Baby Don't Get Hooked On Me
6. City Of New Orleans

Rel: May[4]/
Jun 1975[1]
RRP: £2.55[1]

No tape versions notified to *The New Cassettes & Cartridges* nor *Cassettes & Cartridges*.

DRA sequence 7" singles

Early singles were released via Island and many – if not all – of these would have had no more than one pressing run, though unsold stock may later have been distributed by Mooncrest. At switchover there must have been a large number of pre–existing 7" label blanks because singles from (most likely) DRA 1013 to (almost certainly) DRA 1026 have Island credits inexpertly blacked out with "Manufactured by Mooncrest Records Ltd" text printed above. Later on new label blanks were printed with "Marketed by B&C Records" in line with other B&C–related labels. So far only DRA 1013 has come to light with original Island credits on some copies and the overprinted Mooncrest credits on others, though it is possible that earlier releases still on catalogue may also have had credits overprinted. All that can be said is that none have come to light during research. The earlier run of Island–era singles are listed, not just for the sake of completeness, but because the majority were still available via Mooncrest and later, following the demise of the original Mooncrest, unsold stock, via the resurrected Trojan – those Island releases later available via Trojan have this noted. Oddly, at least one early release was reissued by Polydor during the Mooncrest era. All singles viewed have 4–prong die–cut centres, except DRA 1024 and DRA 1034, which are confirmed only with solid centres. At least some releases were pressed up with the same track on both sides for promotional use as per B&C practice. In line with other labels, this is not documented in these listings.

Island–era releases

DRA 1001   **HOPETOWN LEWIS:** City Of New Orleans / The Wind Cries Mary
Rel: 23 Mar 1973[3]
Reissued on Polydor in April 1974[5].

DRA 1002   **THE SCORPION WITH THE BORIS GARDINER HAPPENING:** Deadly Sting / **THE BORIS GARDINER HAPPENING:** Boing Boing
Rel: 9 Mar 1973[3]
Later available via the resurrected Trojan label[5].

DRA 1003   **KEN PARKER:** Will The Circle Be Unbroken / **THE DYNAMITES:** Will The Circle Be Unbroken (instrumental)
Rel: 9 Mar 1973[3]
Later available via the resurrected Trojan label[5].

DRA 1004   **HENRY AND LIZA:** Hole Under Cratches / **TIVOLIS:** Hole Under Cratches (Instrumental)
Rel: 23 Mar 1973[3]
Later available via the resurrected Trojan label[5].

DRA 1005   NO RELEASE

DRA 1006   **THE CLARENDONIANS:** Walking Up A One Way Street / **THE DYNAMITES:** Walking Up A One Way Street (Instrumental)
Rel: 13 Apr 1973[3]

DRA 1007   **TOOTS AND THE MAYTELS:** Sit Right Down / Screwface Underground / Pomps And Pride
Rel: 20 Apr 1973[3]
Two tracks on b–side. Later available via the resurrected Trojan label[5].

DRA 1008   **BYRON LEE AND THE DRAGONAIRES:** In The Mood / Black On
Rel: 13 Apr 1973[3]
Listed as later available via the resurrected Trojan label[5].

DRA 1009   **ADINA EDWARDS:** Why Don't You Write Me / Just A Closer Walk With Thee
Rel: 11 May 1973[3]

DRA 1010   **JIMMI LONDON:** Jennie / I Wonder If I Care As Much
Rel: 11 May 1973[3]
Later available via the resurrected Trojan label[5].

DRA 1011   HOPETOWN LEWIS: Groovin' Out On Life / God Bless Whoever Sent You
Rel: 1 Jun 1973[3]
Later available via the resurrected Trojan label[5].

DRA 1012   FREDDIE McKAY: Our Rendez–Vous / Black Beauty
Rel: 1 Jun 1973[3]
Later available via the resurrected Trojan label[5].

DRA 1013   TOOTS AND THE MAYTELS: Country Road / Funky Kingston
Rel: 13 Jul 1973[3]
Copies exist with both original Island credits and with Island credits blocked out and Mooncrest credits added. The release date above represents the original Island release just a month in advance of the switch to Mooncrest. Later available via the resurrected Trojan label[5].

DRA 1014   STRANGER AND GLADYS: Conqueror / Conqueror (Instrumental Version)
Rel: 13 Jul[3]/Aug 1973[5]
Release originally advised for July, so the August date may represent the repromotion by Mooncrest.

Mooncrest–era releases

DRA 1015   KEN PARKER: Say Wonderful Things / It's True
Rel: 26 Oct 1973[3]

DRA 1016   TOOTS AND THE MAYTELS: In The Dark / Sailing On
Rel: 9 Nov[3]/30 Nov 1973[3]

DRA 1017   ERIC DONALDSON: What A Festival / Version Festival
Rel: 9 Nov 1973[3]

DRA 1018   ERIC DONALDSON: The Way You Do The Things You Do / Version
Rel: 16 Nov 1973[3]

DRA 1019   JIMMY LONDON: No Letter Today / The Road Is Rough
Rel: 29 Mar 1974[3]
Credited here as "Jimmy" (with a "y"). Later available via the resurrected Trojan label[5].

DRA 1020   ERIC DONALDSON: Watch What You Are Doing To Me / You Must Believe
Rel: 29 Mar 1974[3]

DRA 1021   MAYTELS: Fever / It Was Written Down
Rel: 5 Apr 1974[8]

DRA 1022   FREDDIE McKAY: Dream My Life Over / YOUTH STARS: Version
Rel: 19 Apr 1974[3]

DRA 1023   ERIC DONALDSON: Beautiful Maiden / THE DYNAMITES: Version
Rel: 28 Jun 1974[3]

DRA 1024   THE MAYTELS: Time Tough / Version
Rel: not notified to *The New Singles*
Only solid centred copies confirmed.

DRA 1025 **TINGA STEWART: The Message / Dub**
Rel: not notified to *The New Singles*

DRA 1026 **TOOTS AND THE MAYTELS: Sailing On / If You Act This Way**
Rel: 15 Nov 1974[3]
This is the last confirmed release on overprinted Island label blanks.

DRA 1027 **ERIC DONALDSON: A Weh We A Go Do / SOUL DEFENDERS: A Weh We A Go Do (Part 2)**
Rel: 15 Nov 1974[3]
Confirmed as the joint first release, along with DRA 1028, with the amended "Marketed by B&C" credit on labels. Somehow, DRA 1029, released the same day, slipped out with no distribution credits.

DRA 1028 **MAX ROMEO: No Joshua No / Instrumental**
Rel: 15 Nov 1974[3]

DRA 1029 **THE JAMAICANS: My Heart Just Keeps On Breaking / My Heart Just Keeps On Breaking (Instrumental)**
Rel: 15 Nov 1974[3]
No distribution credits on labels.

DRA 1030 **NORRIS WEIR: Reggay Revolution / Reggae Revolution II**
Rel: 22 Nov 1974[3]
Only solid centred copies confirmed.

DRA 1031 **TELLERS: A–Ya–It–Deh / ENGINEERS: A–Hit–Dub**
Rel: 22 Nov 1974[3]

DRA 1032 **THE ETHIOPIANS: Knowledge Is Power / Power Version**
Rel: 14 Feb 1975[3] (del: 1977[5])

DRA 1033 **BOBBY ELLIS: Up Park Camp / Verse 4**
Rel: 14 Feb 1975[3] (del: 1977[5])

DRA 1034 **ROBERTA SWEED: Words (Are Impossible) / THE DYNAMITES: Words (Are Impossible)**
Rel: 14 Mar 1975[3]
Only solid centred copies confirmed.

Sussex

The majority of LPs on Sussex were back catalogue from the US Sussex label and were issued in November 1974. Most had previously been available in the UK via A&M and, despite supposed deletion, these were still freely available for many years, which must have confused the issue. Sussex received a bit of a 'double whammy' in 1975 with both B&C's liquidation and the shutting down of the US Sussex label for non payment of tax. Most releases were therefore deleted in 1975. A few LPs were listed as still available until 1976 with some singles and tape versions of albums listed as 1977 deletions (and one or two listed as still on catalogue as at 1979). These would most likely have represented original unsold stock and were, by that time, distributed via the resurrected Trojan label.

LPSX sequence LPs

LPSX 1 BILL WITHERS: Still Bill
1. Lonely Town, Lonely Street
2. Let Me In Your Life
3. Who Is He (And What Is He to You)?
4. Use Me
5. Lean On Me

1. Kissing My Love
2. I Don't Know
3. Another Day To Run
4. I Don't Want You On My Mind
5. Take It All In And Check It All Out

Rel: Nov 1974[1/4]
RRP: £2.45[1]
Del: 1975[5]

No tape versions notified to *The New Cassettes & Cartridges* nor *Cassettes & Cartridges*.

LPSX 2 BILL WITHERS: +'Justments
1. You
2. The Same Love That Made Me Laugh
3. Stories
4. Green Grass
5. Ruby Lee

1. Heartbreak Road
2. Can We Pretend
3. Liza
4. Make A Smile For Me
5. Railroad Man

Rel: Nov 1974[1/4]
RRP: £2.45[1]
Del: 1975[5]

Cassette: ZCSUS 2
8–track: Y8SUS 2

Rel: Dec 1974[2]
Rel: Dec 1974[2] (del: 1977[5])

RRP: £2.65[2]
RRP: £2.65[2]

LPSX 3 BILL WITHERS: Just As I Am
1. Harlem
2. Ain't No Sunshine
3. Grandma's Hands
4. Sweet Wanomi
5. Everybody's Talkin'
6. Do It Good

1. Hope She'll Be Happier
2. Let It Be
3. I'm Her Daddy
4. In My Heart
5. Moanin' And Groanin'
6. Better Off Dead

Rel: Nov 1974[1/4]
RRP: £2.45[1]
Del: 1975[5]

No tape versions notified to *The New Cassettes & Cartridges* nor *Cassettes & Cartridges*.

LPSX 4 THE SOUL SEARCHERS: Salt Of The Earth
1. I Rolled It You Hold It
2. Blow Your Whistle
3. Close To You
4. Funk To The Folks

1. Ain't It Heavy
2. Windsong
3. Ashley's Roachclip
4. We Share
5. If It Ain't Funky

Rel: Nov 1974[1/4]
RRP: £2.45[1]
Del: 1975[5]

Cassette: ZCSUS 4
8–track: Y8SUS 4

Rel: Dec 1974[2]
Rel: Dec 1974[2] (del: 1977[5])

RRP: £2.65[2]
RRP: £2.65[2]

The B&C Discography: 1968 to 1975

LPSX 5   MASTERFLEET: High On The Sea

1. First Voyage
2. Skull Stone (To The Bone)
3. Let Love Stand
4. Man And Child
5. Well Phase I

1. Malfunction
2. Academy Awards
3. When You're A New Born
4. Until Tomorrow
5. Well Phase II

Rel: Nov 1974[1/4]
RRP: £2.45[1]

No tape versions notified to *The New Cassettes & Cartridges* nor *Cassettes & Cartridges*.

LPSX 6   CREATIVE SOURCE: Creative Force

1. You Can't Hide Love
2. Let Me In Your Life
3. Lovesville
4. You're Too Good To Be True
5. Wild Flower

1. Magic Carpet Ride
2. Who Is He And What Is He To You
3. Oh Love

Rel: Nov 1974[1/4]
RRP: £2.45[1]
Del: 1976[5]

Cassette: ZCSUS 6   **Rel:** Dec 1974[2] (del: 1977[5])   **RRP:** £2.65[2]
8–track: Y8SUS 6   **Rel:** Dec 1974[2]   **RRP:** £2.65[2]

LPSX 7   CREATIVE SOURCE: Migration

1. I'm Gonna Get There
2. Harlem
3. I Just Can't See Myself Without You

1. Keep On Movin'
2. Migration
3. Corazon
4. Let Me Be The One

Rel: Nov 1974[1/4]
RRP: £2.45[1]
Del: 1976[5]

Cassette: ZCSUS 7   **Rel:** Feb 1975[2] (del: 1977[5])   **RRP:** £2.65[2]
8–track: Y8SUS 7   **Rel:** Feb 1975[2]   **RRP:** £2.65[2]

LPSX 8   LONETTE McKEE: Lonette

1. Message From The Earth
2. You Mean A Lot To Me
3. Save It (Don't Give It Away)
4. I'm Alone
5. Lay Me Down Easy

1. Love Won't Come Easy
2. Do To Me
3. See Ourselves, Be Ourselves, Free Ourselves
4. The Way I Want To Touch You
5. To Whom It May Concern

Rel: Feb 1975[4]
RRP: unknown

Cassette: ZCSUS 8   **Rel:** Mar 1975[2] (del: 1977[5])   **RRP:** £2.65[2]
8–track: Y8SUS 8   **Rel:** Mar 1975[2] (del: 1977[5])   **RRP:** £2.65[2]

LPSX 9   DENNIS COFFEY: Instant Coffee

1. Sonata
2. Moon Star
3. Theme From Enter The Dragon

1. Chicano
2. A Time For Love
3. Kathy
4. Outrageous (The Mind Excursion)

Rel: Apr 1975[1]
RRP: £2.25[1]

No tape versions notified to *The New Cassettes & Cartridges* nor *Cassettes & Cartridges*.

LPSX 10   BILL WITHERS: The Best Of Bill Withers

1. Lean On Me
2. Grandma's Hands
3. Harlem
4. Use Me
5. Everybody's Talkin'

1. Ain't No Sunshine
2. Kissing My Love
3. You
4. The Same Love That Made Me Laugh
5. Who Is He (And What Is He To You)

Rel: Apr 1975[1/4]
RRP: £2.25[1]
Del: 1975[5]

Cassette: ZCSUS 10   **Rel:** May 1975[2]   **RRP:** £2.65[2]
8–track: Y8SUS 10   **Rel:** May 1975[2] (del: 1977[5])   **RRP:** £2.65[2]

LPDX sequence double LP

LPDX 101 **BILL WITHERS: "Live" At Carnegie Hall**

Record 1, side 1
1. Use One
2. Friend Of Mine
3. Ain't No Sunshine
4. Grandma's Hands (With Rap)

Record 1, side 2
1. World Keeps Going Around
2. Let Me In Your Life (With Rap)
3. Better Off Dead
4. For My Friend

Rel: Nov 1974[1/4]
RRP: £2.45[1]
Del: 1975[5]

Record 2, side 1
1. Can't Write Left Handed
2. Lean On Me
3. Lonely Town Lonely Street
4. Hope She'll Be Happier

Record 2, side 2
1. Let Us Love
2. Harlem/Cold Baloney

The RRP in *The New Records* is probably wrong. More likely, this was around £3.49. No tape versions notified to *The New Cassettes & Cartridges* nor *Cassettes & Cartridges*.

SSX sequence 7" singles

SSX 1 **CREATIVE SOURCE: Who Is He And What Is He To You (Vocal) / Who Is He And What Is He To You (Instrumental)**
Rel: 27 Sep 1974[3]

SSX 2 **SOUL SEARCHERS: Blow Your Whistle / Funk To The Folks**
Rel: 4 Oct 1974[3]

SSX 3 **MASTER FLEET: Well Phase I / Well Phase II**
Rel: 4 Oct 1974[3]

SSX 4 **LONETTE McKEE: Save It (Don't Give It Away) / Do To Me**
Rel: not notified to *The New Singles*
Also rumoured to exist with b–side titled "Do It To Me", though this is unconfirmed.

SSX 5 **CREATIVE SOURCE: Migration / Keep On Movin'**
Rel: 3 Jan 1975[3] (del: 1977[5])

SSX 6 **DENNIS COFFEE: Getting It On '75 / Chicano**
Rel: 24 Jan 1975[3] (del: 1977[5])

SSX 7 **BILL WITHERS: Heartbreak Road / Ruby Lee**
Rel: 7 Feb 1975[3]

SSX 8 **GALLERY: I Belive In Music / Louisina Line**
Rel: 4 Apr 1975[3] (del: 1977[5])

SSX 9 **BILL WITHERS: Lean On Me / Use Me**
Rel: 11 Apr 1975[3]

Seven Sun

A bit of a sad one, this. The Seven Sun label was originally distributed by President Records and released thirteen singles and at least one (extremely valuable) LP between February 1972 and September 1974. There was a hiatus during which distribution switched to B&C. At least two of the first three B&C releases were scheduled for late June 1975 release, just in time to be swallowed up in B&C's liquidation. All copies viewed have a very large "A" printed on the a–side – does this denote that they are promotional copies? Or was this just to give a big hint as to which side they wanted deejays to play? If the former, perhaps no normal stock copies were ever pressed. Does anyone know?

SSUN sequence 7" singles

SSUN 14   *NORMAN BEATON: Love Is Around / The Skin*
Rel: 20 Jun 1975[3]

SSUN 15   *100% PROOF: Kisses Kisses Kisses / He's The Guy*
Rel: 20 Jun 1975[3]

SSUN 16   *BLACK VELVET: I'm On My Way / Groove Along*
Rel: not notified to *The New Singles*

And Finally...

... well, to be strictly accurate, the Seven Sun label came last, datewise, but at least copies of all three singles on that label are confirmed as existing (whether they got as far as the shops or not is another matter), whereas no copies of either cassette or 8–track copy of this album have come to light, though this doesn't mean that it doesn't exist.

Anyway, to the album. It's April 1975 and it is obvious that the ship is sinking. What to do? How about putting out a special, cross–label greatest hits package. Okay, but just what audience is this particular selection aimed at? Ronco and K–tel album buyers by the look of it – all it does is to pull together the B&C Group's highest–charting hits, but with no real attempt at consistency of style – moving from hard rock to rock steady to singalong folk pop to progressive rock to soul – and that's just the first six tracks.

As already mentioned, whether this got as far as the shops is unknown, but it was advised to both Francis Antony and *Music Master* – it was listed in the May 1975 edition of *The New Cassettes & Cartridges* as a B&C label release – but adverts in the music press seem to be conspicuous by their absence. On the other hand, there are deletion dates for both tape formats in *Music Master*, which lists the late distributor as the resurrected Trojan. This does not necessarily mean that the album existed in any form other than on paper – as with Moon 51, this might just represent the point at which Trojan got fed up with being asked for something that didn't exist and formally deleted it.

Lots of B&C labels are represented here: Mooncrest – Nazareth and Hotshots; Charisma – Rare Bird, Lindisfarne, Genesis, Gary Shearston and The Nice; People – Don Downing; B&C – Atomic Rooster; Trojan – Jimmy Cliff, Greyhound, John Holt and Ken Boothe; Harry J – Bob and Marcia; Horse – Scott English. The Desmond Dekker and the Aces track was a hit on Pyramid, distributed by Doctor Bird, but the label later became part of the B&C Group. The Bill Withers track was a hit on A&M, but the track was currently licensed to B&C via the Sussex label. There was also a bit of cheating going on with The Nice track because this was not the hit version, but was a live version. Well, okay, the live version was from a hit LP, if you want to be pedantic, but the hit single it wasn't!

A last–ditch cross–label tape–only hits package

ZCB 551/Y8BC 551   VARIOUS ARTISTS: High Powered Hits

1. Broken Down Angel (Nazareth)
2. Isrealites (Desmond Dekker)
3. Lady Eleanor (Lindisfarne)
4. I Know What I Like (Genesis)
5. Black And White (Greyhound)
6. Lean On Me (Bill Withers)
7. Wonderful World, Beautiful People (Jimmy Cliff)
8. Young, Gifted And Black (Bob and Marcia)
9. I Get A Kick Out Of You (Gary Shearston)
10. Gaye (Clifford T. Ward)

1. Meet Me On The Corner (Lindisfarne)
2. Sympathy (Rare Bird)
3. Help Me Make It Through The Night (John Holt)
4. Lonely Days Lonely Nights (Don Downing)
5. America (The Nice)
6. Tomorrow Night (Atomic Rooster)
7. Snoopy Vs. The Red Baron (Hotshots)
8. This Flight Tonight (Nazareth)
9. Brandy (Scott Englilsh)
10. Everything I Own (Ken Boothe)

Rel: May 1975[2]
RRP: £2.65[2]
Del: 1977[5]

It is the purest guesswork that there were ten tracks on each side. *America* would almost certainly have been an edited version, possibly as per later issue on Charisma's *Repeat Performance* LP.

The Great British Record Label series

Every book in the Great British Record Label series has received a great deal of praise thanks to a combination of attention to detail and the fact that the author's knowledge and love of British record labels both mainstream and oddball shines through. The intention was – and remains – to make each book in the series the definitive work on the label. *Bristol Folk*, by the same author, predates this series, but already pointed the way!

The Famous Charisma Discography

The first book in the series was produced to celebrate the 40th anniversary of Charisma, possibly the greatest independent British record label that has ever existed. Tony Stratton Smith, the label's owner, used his maxim of "Anything good of its kind" to put together an enviable roster of artists as diverse as Genesis, Van der Graaf Generator, Sir John Betjeman, John Arlott, Malcolm McLaren, Bo Hansson, Lindisfarne and Hawkwind.

Paperback: ISBN 978–0–9563531–1–5/Kindle: ISBN 978–0–9563531–4–6   ePub version coming soon

The Saydisc and Village Thing Discography

This discography provides an in–depth view of the wonderfully–eclectic Saydisc label and related Village Thing, Matchbox, Roots, Amon Ra and Ahura Mazda labels. The release celebrated the 45th anniversary of Saydisc and the 40th anniversary of Village Thing, the original 'folkadelia' label, and the author was given special access to the label archives. The book includes access to many previously–unpublished photographs.

Paperback: ISBN 978–0–9563531–2–2   Kindle and ePub versions coming soon*

Transacord: Sounds of Steam (with free limited edition CD)

Possibly Britain's best–loved specialist label, Transacord was run by the celebrated British Film Sound Recordist, Peter Handford. The label started life in 1953 and released its first railway recording in 1955. The heyday was in the 1960s, when Argo took over the business end of things and Transacord records started selling in silly quantities. The book includes a limited edition, free CD with two tracks never before available on CD.

Paperback: ISBN 978–0–9563531–3–9   Kindle and ePub versions coming soon*

Bristol Folk: a Discographical History

Bristol Folk has proved very popular with fans of British folk, blues and 'psych' or 'acid folk'. Why Bristol? Well, Bristol's nationally recognised folk scene was a magnet for established names, such as Al Stewart, Stefan Grossman, the Incredible String Band and John Renbourn, whilst Bristol's own enviable roster of artists included Ian Anderson, Pigsty Hill Light Orchestra, Adge Cutler and the Wurzels, Shelagh McDonald, Stackridge, Al Jones, Steve Tilston, Dave Evans, Keith Christmas, and more. 34 pages of illustrations include record sleeves, photographs (many previously unpublished), promotional materials and memorabilia from private collections and archives to which the author had special access. Fred Wedlock contributed a postscript shortly before his untimely death.

Paperback: ISBN 978–0–9563531–0–8   Kindle and ePub versions coming soon*

Coming soon

Volumes in the pipeline cover Virgin, Harvest, Manticore, Purple, Swan Song, Immediate, WWA, Nepentha and others. One day the author will tackle Vertigo, Island, Topic, Transatlantic and the Trojan series of labels if he lives long enough.

All available from www.bristol–folk.co.uk
*digital versions are text only

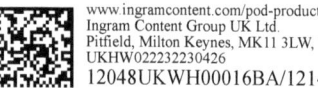
www.ingramcontent.com/pod-product-compliance
Ingram Content Group UK Ltd.
Pitfield, Milton Keynes, MK11 3LW, UK
UKHW022232230426
12048UKWH00016BA/1214